Sandy Creek
NEW YORK

An Imprint of Sterling Publishing
387 Park Avenue South
New York, NY 10016

Text © 2013 by QEB Publishing, Inc.
Illustrations © 2013 by QEB Publishing, Inc.

This 2013 edition published by Sandy Creek.

Design: Dave Ball @ D&A

ISBN: 978-1-4351-4403-3

Manufactured in Guangdong, China
Lot #:
2 4 6 8 10 9 7 5 3
06/13

Picture Credits

ardea.com: Francois Gohier 108,

Corbis: Alissa Crandrall 10b, Jim Zuckerman 14b, John Conrad 14-15, Tom Brakefield 15t, Alan & Sandy Carey/ Zefra 18-19, Jim Zuckerman 24b, Cyril Ruoso 34-35, D. Robert & Lorri Franz 37t, 38, David A. Northcott 41b, Tom Brakefield 46-47, Christophe Loviny 52, Eric & David Hosking 63b, Philip Richardson 64-65, Joe McDonald 65b, Ron Austing 69, Fritz Polking 72-73, Robert Pickett 94-95, 95b, Amos Nachoum 100-101, Brandon D Cole 111b, Flip Nicklin 114-115, Theo Allofs 116-117, Joe McDonald 119t, Corbis 123b, Malcolm Kitto 123t,

Ecoscene: Tom Ang 18b, R Pickett 26, 30-31, 122b, 131t, Jamie Harron 40-41, Fritz Polking 41t, 70b, Michael Gore 42b, Fritz Polking 65t, John Pitcher 67t, Kjell Sandved 72b, John Lewis 101t, Chinch Gryniewwicz 101, 130-131, Philip Colla 103b, 113b, Ken Wilson 121, Kieran Murray 131b, Sally Morgan 131b

FLPA: ImageBroker 8-9, Imagebroker 16-17, 107t, Kevin Schafer 35b, Lydie Gigerichova 35t, David Hosking 39b, Stanley Breeden 45t, Mark Raycroft 45b, Gary K Smitj 47t, Grzegorz Lesniewski 48-49, Hugo Wilcox 49t, Derek Middleton 49b, Foto Natura 50-51, Terry Whittaker 54-55, Nigel Dowsett 55c, Jurgen & Christine Sohns 56-57, Image Broker 57t, Paul Hobson 59t, 60-61 Photo Researchers, Scott Linstead 61t, Richard Brooks 68, Pete Oxford 97t, Michael & Patricia Fogden 99t, Imagebroker 104b, Conger Eel 106b, Norbert Probst 106-107, Frank W Lane 109t, Gerard Lacz 110, Mike Parry 111t, Konrad Wothe 120-121, Gail Shumway 126-127, Bill Coster 134b, Derek Middleton 136b,

Getty: Gail Shumway 11t, 130T Anup Shah 15b, Martin Harvey 20, Jack Hollingsworth 26-27, Stan Osolinski 27b, Daryl Balfour 28, Johan Elzenga 28-29, Arte Wolfe 30, 74t, Steve Bloom 33t, David E. Meyers 42-43, Wayne R. Bilenduke 43t, Arte Wolfe 50b, Konrad Wothe 51t, Michael & Patricia Fogden 52-53, Grant Faint 62-63, Johnny Johnson 70-71, Joseph Van Os 71, Wolfgang Kaehler 73, Mike Hill 74b, Paul Souders 75t, David Tipling 75b, Joe Blossom 93b, Jeff Rotman 102b, Jeff Hunter 102-103, Docwhite 108-109, Flip Nicklin 113t, Carol Farneti 122-123, Al Satterwhite 124-125, Tischenko Irina Royal Background 128-129, Michael Durham 141t, Kathy Bushue 142, Linda Pitkin 144

NHPA: Kevin Schafer 22-23, 23t, John Shaw 23b, Daryl Balfour 25t, Andy Rouse 36-37, Ernie Janes 37b, Melvin Grey 51b, Stephen Dalton 53t, 118b, 120b, Oxford Scientific 53b, Jordi bas Casas 67b

NPL: Doug Perrine 105b

Photolibrary: Renee Lynn 20-21

Shutterstock: Jim Agronick 4b, Szefei 4-5, PRILL 5t, Eduard Kyslynskyy 6-7, Covenant 7t, Susan Flashman 7b, Matt Cooper 9t, 12qwerty 9b, Paul Vorwerk 19b, Valdecasas 21t, Maggy Meyer 21b, Uryanikov Sergey 24-25, Vladimir Wrangel 40t, Selenznev Oleg 44, Frantisek Czanner 47b, Jeff Banke 54b, Citterbiz 55t, Wolfgang Kruck 55b, Janelle Lugge 56b, Steve Byland 57b, Grant Glendinning 58-59, Anmor Photography 59b, Meskal 61b, Miorenz 66, Dr. Morley Read 92t, Matt Jeppson 96-97, Jason Patrick Ross 96-97b, WitR 98-99, FAUP 100b, totophotos 104-105, Manda Nicholls 105t, Karisa Hess 112b, Kristian Sekulic 112-113, Jan Van der Hoeven 114b, Wolfgang Amri 115, Natalie Jean 116, Vladimir Melnik 117b, Jan Martin Will 117t, Kirsanov 124b, Audrey Snider-Bell, Tyler Fox 132-133, Gtranquillity 135t, illiuta goean 135b, NH 136-137, Alexey Stiop 137b, EcoPrint 138-139, Henrik Larsson 139b

Stillpictures: BIOS 10-11, Martin Harvey 13, Michel Gunther 31t, Martin Harvey 32-33, John Cancalosi 36b, Evelyn Gallardo 39t, Gunter Ziesler 63t

CONTENTS

Words in **bold** are explained in the Glossary on page 140.

WHAT IS AN ANIMAL?

Animals can be divided into two main groups: vertebrates (animals with backbones) and invertebrates (animals without backbones). **Mammals**, birds, **reptiles**, **amphibians**, and fish all have backbones, while **insects**, spiders and molluscs do not.

A butterfly is an insect, the most common type of animal on Earth.

A shark is a type of fish. It takes oxygen from water rather than air.

Habitats around the world

Animals live everywhere on Earth—from hot, dry deserts and open grassland to freezing polar regions and deep oceans. An animal's natural home or environment is called its **habitat**. Most animals are adapted to live in only one or two habitats. Some animals **migrate** in the autumn to find warmer habitats with more food.

A giraffe is a mammal Giraffes are plant-eaters, but some mammals feed on other animals.

Signs of life

There are seven main "signs of life" that distinguish living things from non-living objects. All animals...

Breathe to get oxygen into the body

Reproduce to make new individuals

Move around to find food, mates, or escape danger

Feed to make new energy for the body

Sense the world around them by sight, smell, touch, hearing, and taste

Grow to reach their full size

Excrete to remove waste from the body.

MARSUPIALS

Most marsupials live in Australia. The word marsupial means "pouched mammal". The young are born at a very underdeveloped stage. Once born, the babies must make their way to a furry pouch on the mother's body to develop in safety.

A kangaroo can make huge leaps and reach speeds of up to 35 miles per hour.

Red kangaroo

The red kangaroo is the largest marsupial. It bounds along on its back legs. It lives in Australia's hot deserts and grasslands. The female gives birth to a single baby called a joey.

Koala

The koala spends up to 18 hours each day asleep. The rest of the time it feeds on the leaves of eucalyptus trees, rarely leaving the trees. Special pouches in its cheeks store the leaves until it needs to eat them.

A koala lives in dry forests in eastern Austraila.

FANTASTIC FACT

When a Tasmanian devil gets angry, its ears turn bright red!

Tasmanian devil

The Tasmanian devil has a reputation as a vicious **predator**. It is about the size of a small dog and has powerful jaws that enable it to crush the bones of its prey. It feeds on reptiles, birds, fish, and small mammals.

A Tasmanian devil's cry is a loud, blood-curdling screech!

WILD DOGS

All domestic dogs are descended from wolves. Wolves and other wild dogs have long legs for chasing prey and sharp teeth for killing it.

The pack leader is called the alpha male.

Gray wolf

The largest of all the wild dogs, the gray wolf preys on animals such as bison, moose, and musk-oxen. Gray wolves hunt in packs that are led by the strongest male. The wolves will howl loudly to warn other packs to stay away.

FANTASTIC FACT
A gray wolf pack's hunting **territory** can cover up to 386 square miles.

Coyotes

Coyotes live on prairies and open woodland in North and Central America. A coyote's diet consists mainly of rodents and rabbits, although it will also eat snakes and insects!

A coyote will grow up to three feet long.

A baby fox is called a kit.

Red fox

The red fox has adapted to many different environments, from forests and grasslands to mountains, deserts, and even cities. Red foxes live and hunt alone and come together only to breed and rear their young.

LIONS

A mane protects a lion's neck during a fight.

A lion is a big cat and related to tigers, cheetahs, and leopards. All these cats are skillful hunters that eat meat.

Lions and lionesses

It is easy to identify a male lion, as he has a thick mane around his head. A female lion is known as a lioness, and her young are called cubs. Both lions and lionesses live together in families called prides.

A lioness will give birth to up to four cubs.

FANTASTIC FACT

The lion's tongue is like sandpaper. It is used to scrape bits of meat off bones.

Lion types

There is only one **species**, or type, of lion. However, there are slight variations between lions living in different parts of the world. They are divided into five groups called subspecies. They are the Angolan, Asiatic, Masai, Senegalese, and Transvaal lions.

All subspecies of lion live in Africa, except the Asiatic lions.

Asiatic lions

Asiatic lions are very rare, living in just one forest in India. There are several differences between the Asiatic lion and the African lion. The Asiatic lion has a longer tassel on its tail and a tuft of hair on each elbow.

An Asiatic lion has a shorter mane and a thicker coat than the African lion.

HUNTING LIONS

Lions cannot run for long distances. They must quickly rush in for the kill

The lionesses do most of the hunting. They are strong enough to kill prey that is as large as they are. Their claws are long, strong, and curved to hook into their prey's flesh.

A lion's large eyes glow in the dark, like a pet cat's do.

Excellent eyesight

A lion's eyes are the largest of any cat. They point forward and this helps them to judge distances well. This is especially useful when a lion is chasing and leaping onto prey.

Hunting together

At the start of a hunt, lionesses spread out in a fan shape. Some walk toward the prey, forcing it toward other lionesses that are hidden in the grass. These lionesses ambush the prey when it draws near.

This pride of lions has brought down a buffalo.

FANTASTIC FACT

Lions often share their territory with other predators, such as cheetahs and leopards.

Silent walking

Lions can walk almost silently. Under each toe there is a pad that cushions their paws and softens any noise. Their claws can be pulled back, or retracted, inside their toes when they are not being used.

Lions have pads on their paws that help them to creep up on their prey.

TIGERS

The tiger is the largest cat in the world. It is easy to recognize, with its coat of red-orange and dark stripes. The tiger is a **carnivore**; this means that it eats other animals.

Unlike some big cats, tigers like to live alone.

FANTASTIC FACT
The largest known Siberian tiger weighed 1,027 pounds!

Tiger types

There is only one species of tiger. This species is divided into five subspecies. These are the Sumatran, Siberian or Amur, Bengal or Indian, South China, and Indo-Chinese tigers.

White Bengal tigers are rare. Most of them have blue eyes!

Tiger habitats

All tigers live in Asia. Some tigers live in countries where it gets very cold, like in parts of North Korea, eastern Russia, and China. Other tigers live where the climate is warmer, such as India and parts of Southeast Asia.

The Siberian tiger has thick fur to keep it warm during the cold Siberian winters.

If a male tiger enters another male's territory, there is usually a fight. The winner will take over the territory.

Living alone

Tigers live alone in an area called a territory. Territories differ in size and can be fairly small if there's plenty of prey to be found. Both male and female tigers may have their own territory.

CARNIVOROUS TIGERS

Tigers are carnivores, which means that they eat other animals. They prey on large, hoofed mammals, such as deer. Tigers have strong, hooked claws that allow the tiger to grip its prey and pull it to the ground.

FANTASTIC FACT

Tigers are skillful hunters but still only one in every 10 or 20 attempts to catch prey is successful.

Tiger teeth

Tigers have powerful jaws. They have small incisor teeth at the front of the mouth to grip prey and pull meat, four sharp canine teeth for stabbing, and large teeth called molars at the back of the mouth for chewing meat and bone.

Tigers have huge shoulders for lifting and dragging prey.

An adult tiger has 30 teeth.

Learning to hunt

Cubs watch their mother hunt and kill prey. As they get older, the mother catches prey and allows her cubs to kill it. Eventually, they practice hunting on their own, starting with small prey, such as birds and rodents.

Play-fighting is important, as it helps young cubs learn to hunt.

Tiger hearing

A tiger's hearing is its best sense. A tiger can tell the difference between leaves rustling in the breeze and the sound of an animal brushing through the undergrowth.

Sight and hearing are the tiger's most important senses.

17

CHEETAHS

The cheetah is the fastest land animal in the world. It is a large, slim, long-legged cat with a spotted coat. The cheetah's closest relatives are the other big cats, including the lion, tiger, and leopard.

Different cheetahs

There is one species of cheetah, but there are small differences between cheetahs living in different parts of the world. The desert cheetah of the Sahara has a much paler coat than most other cheetahs. This helps it blend with the color of desert sand. Because of these differences, cheetahs are grouped into subspecies. There are three subspecies in Africa and two in Asia.

Cheetahs are attractive animals, but they can be dangerous too.

The Asiatic cheetah's coat is perfectly colored for the grassland in which it lives.

Hunters

Cheetahs are called predators because they hunt and eat other animals. When they hunt together, a family of cheetahs can bring down and kill large prey.

These cheetahs have brought down a water buck.

FAST CHEETAHS

Although an adult cheetah can reach an amazing top speed of more than 62 miles per hour, it usually runs at a slower 37-44 miles per hour when chasing after its prey.

Built for speed

The cheetah's slim body, long legs and bendy back are built for speed. It can take long strides and move across the ground quickly. Large lungs allow the cheetah to breathe plenty of air, and a long tail helps it keep its balance, especially when changing direction.

These cheetahs are seen at full stretch as they lift all four legs off the ground while running fast.

A cheetah's powerful tail helps it stay balanced while turning.

Firm grip

The cheetah's claws are never completely retracted. They help it keep a firm grip on the ground when running.

A cheetah's claws are always visible.

A cheetah must rest after a very fast run.

Running hot

The cheetah gets very hot when running fast, so it can only run at top speed for about one minute. After this, the cheetah has to stop or its body will become too hot.

FANTASTIC FACT

A cheetah can run 328 feet in less than four seconds. This is over twice as fast as any human.

GIRAFFES

The giraffe is the tallest animal in the world. It has an incredibly long neck and four long legs. Its coat has a pattern of brown patches on a lighter, yellowish background.

Each giraffe has it own unique pattern of markings.

Life on the savannah

Giraffes live only in Africa. They live on savannah grasslands. These are vast plains covered in grass. During the dry season, the ground is dry and the grasses are golden yellow. Once the rains come, the grass grows and turns green.

The areas in pink show where giraffes are found.

The coat of the Masai giraffe has a pattern similar to leaves.

Giraffe types

The giraffe species is divided into nine subspecies. Many of these are named after the areas in which they live. For example, the Masai giraffe is from the Masai Mara, in Kenya.

Coat colors

As well as having different patterns, giraffes' coats vary in color too. The color of coat depends on where the giraffe lives as well as the leaves they eat. Giraffes who live in drier, dustier places have paler yellow coats because they have adapted to their surroundings.

The Rothschild's giraffe is from Uganda and northern Kenya. It has deep brown, rectangular spots.

23

BENDING AND STRETCHING

Giraffes are plant-eaters, or **herbivores**. They feed on the leaves of trees. You can tell a male giraffe (bull) from a female giraffe (cow) by the way it eats. Cows tend to bend their necks, while bulls eat at full stretch.

Neck bones

Believe it or not, the long neck of the giraffe has the same number of bones as a person's neck—that's just seven vertebrae. However, each vertebra of the giraffe is much longer than that of a human being.

There are special valves in the blood vessels of the giraffe's neck that stop blood rushing to its head when it bends over.

Drinking danger

Giraffes get most of their water from the leaves they eat, but sometimes they must drink from a river or water hole. To reach down, they move their front feet apart, bend their knees, and lower their necks. This is a very dangerous time for giraffes. It is easy for a predator, such as a crocodile, to grab hold of a giraffe when it is bent over.

A giraffe bends down to drink

Giraffes use their tongues and thick lips to pull leaves into their mouths.

FANTASTIC FACT

The giraffe tongue is very long. It is about 18 inches—that's as long as a child's arm!

ELEPHANTS

The elephant has a huge gray body and strong legs that look like pillars. It has a long trunk instead of the short nose that we have. It also has large flapping ears. Most elephants have tusks too.

A fully grown elephant uses her trunk to feed on grass.

The Asian elephant has small ears and a long face.

Elephant types

There are three species, or types, of elephant. They are the African, African Forest and Asian elephants. The African elephant is the largest of the elephants. It has large ears and long tusks. The Asian elephant has much smaller ears and its skin is less wrinkled.

Spot the difference

The African and African forest elephants appear the same, but there are some differences. The African forest elephant is smaller. It also has a hairy trunk. Its tusks point downwards so that they do not get tangled in vegetation in the forests where it lives.

An African bull elephant.

Living in a herd

Female elephants live in family groups called herds. A typical herd is made up of three or four adult females and their calves. All its adult females are related. The herd is led by the oldest female. She is called the matriarch.

Young elephants learn by watching their mothers and the other members of the herd

FANTASTIC FACT

Both the African bull and female elephants have tusks, but only the Asian bull elephant has tusks.

TRUNKS AND TUSKS

Elephants use their tusks and trunks for lots of things. Tusks are extra long teeth that continue to grow throughout the elephant's life.

An elephant's trunk is long enough to reach into the trees for leaves and fruit.

FANTASTIC FACT

It is almost impossible for an elephant to survive if its trunk is damaged.

Elephants can pick up small objects with the end of their trunks.

A long nose

An elephant uses its trunk to smell things. The trunk is formed from the elephant's nose and upper lip. Smell helps to keep a herd together. It allows elephants to detect predators, such as lions or tigers. Smell also helps elephants find food.

Elephant noises

Elephants make a trumpeting sound with their trunks when they are excited, surprised, or when they are about to attack. They also squeal, cry, scream, roar, snort, and groan!

Elephants use signals, such as a raised trunk, to show anger.

Using their tusks

Elephants use their tusks to dig for food and pull down trees. Baby elephants have tiny milk tusks. These drop out before calves reach two years of age. They are replaced by permanent tusks made of ivory.

An elephant's tusks grow up to 7 inches a year.

GORILLAS

The gorilla is the world's largest **primate**. People are primates, too, and gorillas are one of our closest animal relatives. Gorillas are gentle and clever. Some gorillas in captivity have even learned a few words in sign language.

Gorillas have a large head with a bulging forehead, tiny ears, and small brown eyes.

Types of gorilla

There is only one species of gorilla. However, it is divided into three subspecies, named after the places where they live: the mountain gorilla, the western lowland gorilla, and the eastern lowland gorilla.

FANTASTIC FACT

The name gorilla means 'hairy person'. It was first used by an explorer from North Africa 2,500 years ago.

Spot the difference

Male gorillas are twice as big as female gorillas. Older males have white hair on their backs and are called Silverbacks. The western lowland gorilla also has brown hair, while the mountain gorilla and the eastern lowland gorilla have black hair.

Silverback males are so called because of the white hair shaped like a saddle on their backs.

Mountain gorillas live in chilly forests that are 9,842 feet above sea level.

Gorilla habitats

Wild gorillas live in the forests of Africa. It is hot all year where lowland gorillas live, and it rains almost every day. It is cloudy and cold where mountain gorillas live, so they have long hair to keep them warm.

GORILLA LIFE

Gorillas are omnivores, like people. This means that they eat both animals and plants. Although most of their food is leaves, they also eat fruits, flowers, grass, mushrooms, and small insects. Gorillas do not need to drink, as they get all the water they need from their food.

Gorillas sit in family groups in clearings, playing, eating and grooming.

FANTASTIC FACT

A full-grown male gorilla eats about 48 pounds of food every day.

Family life

Gorillas are too big to move around easily in dense forest, so they sit in family groups of between three and 30 animals. Young gorillas live with their family until they are ten years old. The silverback is head of the group.

Male gorillas show their long canines when angry. They are used for fighting, not eating.

Teeth

Gorillas grow two sets of teeth and have incisors, canines, premolars, and molars, just as humans do. A young gorilla's small **milk teeth** fall out and are replaced by large permanent teeth when it is about three years old.

Eating all day

Family groups move slowly through the forest searching for food in an area of forest called a territory. They eat mainly leaves and roots, which make them feel full quickly, so they sit and rest to digest their food.

33

APES, GIBBONS, AND MONKEYS

Humans, gorillas, monkeys, and apes all belong to a group of 250 species called primates. Many primates have opposable thumbs, which means that their thumbs can move across their palms to grasp objects. Some also have opposable big toes. Many monkeys will use their tails for help when climbing.

This chimpanzee uses its opposable thumbs to make use of simple tools.

Chimpanzee

The chimpanzee makes many noises, gestures, and facial expressions. They mainly eat plants, but they will occasionally eat insects and meat. Chimpanzees have learned to use some objects as simple tools. A stone will help to smash open a nut, and sticks will help to pry grubs from rotten wood.

Mandrill

The forest-dwelling Mandrill is easy to identify. It has a long red nose and blue cheeks. One male guards a group of females while they forage for fruits, nuts, mushrooms, and worms.

The Mandrill has very distinctive, colorful markings.

Red howler monkeys use their tails like an extra leg when climbing.

Red howler monkey

Red howler monkeys live in the **rainforest** in groups of up to 30. The males have a large throat, which has a special chamber that amplifies its call. The howling tells other monkeys to stay away from their territory.

FANTASTIC FACT

Sometimes male howler monkeys join in a chorus of howls that can be heard up to three miles away!

ORANGUTANS

Orangutans are one of our closest primate relatives. Wild orangutans live in rainforests on the islands of Sumatra and Borneo. They are covered in long, orange-red hair and eat mostly plants. More than half of their diet is fruit.

Orangutans move around the rainforest by climbing along branches.

FANTASTIC FACT

Orangutans have very long arms. The length of each arm is about the same as the height of a five-year-old child!

Big and strong

Male orangutans weigh about 176 pounds, twice the weight of the females. Once the male reaches the age of 14, he grows an enormous pouch under his throat. He uses this when he calls. He also grows cheek pads, which are mostly fat.

Adult males have facial hair that looks like a man's moustache and beard.

Spot the difference

There is only one species of orangutan. The orangutans on Sumatra look different from those in Borneo, so they are both called subspecies. Sumatran orangutans are lighter in color, have a longer, narrow face and thicker, longer hair

These Sumatran orangutans are lighter in color than those from Borneo.

Living alone

Orangutans do not live in small groups like most primates. The only time they live with other orangutans is when they are growing up, when a young female returns to visit her mother or when a male visits a female to mate with her.

A baby orangutan drinks milk from its mother until it is three or four years old.

RAINFOREST LIFE

Orangutans live in rainforests. These are very dense forests in places where it is hot and wet almost all year round. The trees grow very close together and block out most of the light from the forest floor.

FANTASTIC FACT

One female orangutan used 54 tools for hunting insects and 20 tools for picking fruit!

Orangutans move slowly and rarely travel more than half a mile in a day.

Orangutan senses

Orangutans have the same five senses as humans. They use their sense of smell to find food. Like other primates, orangutans can see in color, but the rainforest is very dark. Good hearing is important for hearing predators and the calls of other orangutans.

Afternoon nap

In the rainforest, the middle of the day is very hot. Orangutans rise at dawn and move around an area called their home range. They feed for two to three hours, then rest in the branches where they are safe from predators until afternoon, when they start looking for food again.

Orangutans tend to walk on all fours, using their fists for support.

Intelligent animals

Orangutans have learned to use sticks as tools to scratch themselves, dig, and collect food, and to pull out the seeds from a tasty but prickly fruit called a puwin. They also use leaves to make nests, collect drinking water, and for shelter.

Orangutans build a shelter from leaves to hide under during heavy rain.

BEARS

Bears are some of the best-known animals in the world. Bears have a heavy body covered in thick fur. They have large feet called paws that have a long, sharp claw on each toe, and large heads with long noses and small eyes.

The sun bear uses its long tongue to find food.

Brown bears have very thick, dark brown fur.

Types of bear

There are eight species of bear. The most well known are the polar bear, the brown bear (often known as the grizzly) and the giant panda. Less well-known species are the American black bear, the Asian black bear, the sun bear, the sloth bear, and the spectacled bear.

Bear habitats

Bears are only found in certain areas of the world. Polar bears live mainly in the Arctic Circle. Giant pandas live only in the bamboo forests of central China, but brown and black bears can be found across North America, northern Europe, and Asia.

The polar bear is the only completely white bear. This is good camouflage against the snow.

The sloth bear has no front teeth so it can suck termites from their nest.

FANTASTIC FACT

American black bears are not always black. They come in all shades of brown and a few are white!

Other bears

The Asian black bear, sun bear, sloth bear, and spectacled bear are much smaller than the other four types of bear. The sun bear is the smallest. These smaller bears eat a mixed diet of insects, fruits, and honey.

41

HUNTING AND HIBERNATION

Black and brown bears that live in colder areas of the world cannot find enough food during the winter. In autumn, they eat as much food as possible and then spend the cold months in a deep sleep called hibernation.

Bear senses

Polar bears have sharper eyesight than other bears, and can see well underwater. They can smell their prey on the ice many miles away. All bears have a very good sense of smell, as they use it to find food, identify their cubs, and find a mate.

A seal provides enough food to feed a polar bear for about eight days.

FANTASTIC FACT

Bears have been known to detect a human's scent more than 14 hours after the person has walked by.

Frozen hunting ground

Polar bears spend a lot of time hunting on ice. Small, soft bumps on the pads of their paws stop them from slipping. Under their thick fur they have black skin, which absorbs heat. They have a thick layer of fat called **blubber** to keep them warm.

Polar bears do not hibernate. Pregnant females spend the winter in a hole under the snow to have their cubs.

Brown bears catch the slippery salmon in their claws or teeth.

What do bears hunt?

Polar bears and brown bears are predators. They have sharp teeth and long claws to grip their prey. Bear cubs learn how to hunt by watching their mother. Polar bears are carnivores, but brown bears are omnivores and eat fish, insects, and berries, too.

CAMELS, DEER, AND HORSES

The camel's hump helps it survive when food and water are scarce.

Camels and deer have an even number of toes and are cud-chewers. This means they briefly chew leaves and grass, then swallow them. They then bring up this partly digested food from their stomachs and chew it again. Horses have only one toe on each foot, ending in a hoof, so they can run swiftly.

Dromedary camel

The dromedary, or one-humped camel, no longer exists in the wild. It is now just a domesticated animal. It has been bred in two forms: as a heavily built camel for carrying loads and a lighter one for racing. The hump acts as a fat store fro the camel to live on when food is scarce. It can go without water for long periods.

FANTASTIC FACT

A caribou can sniff out lichen that is beneath about five feet of snow!

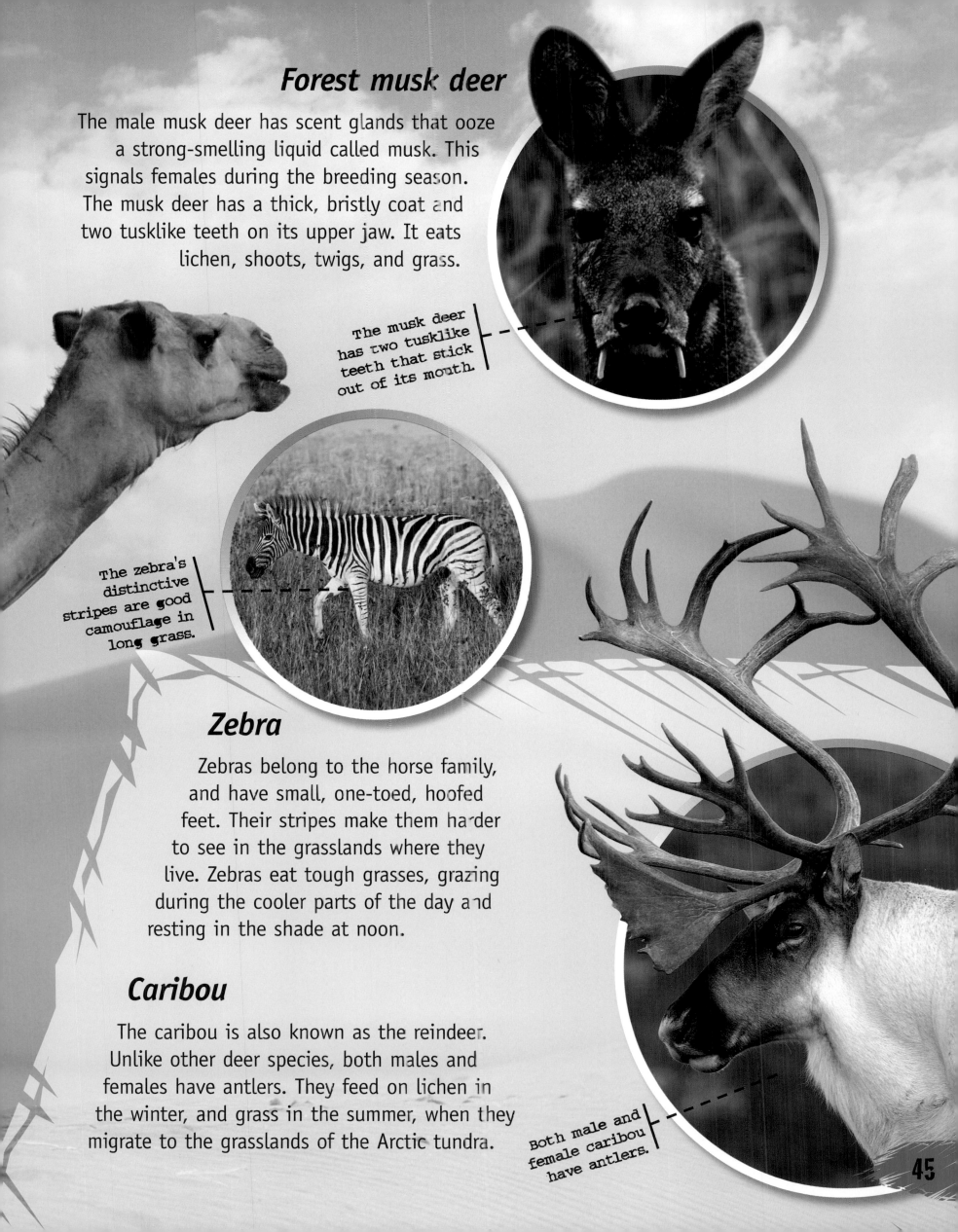

Forest musk deer

The male musk deer has scent glands that ooze a strong-smelling liquid called musk. This signals females during the breeding season. The musk deer has a thick, bristly coat and two tusklike teeth on its upper jaw. It eats lichen, shoots, twigs, and grass.

The musk deer has two tusklike teeth that stick out of its mouth.

The zebra's distinctive stripes are good camouflage in long grass.

Zebra

Zebras belong to the horse family, and have small, one-toed, hoofed feet. Their stripes make them harder to see in the grasslands where they live. Zebras eat tough grasses, grazing during the cooler parts of the day and resting in the shade at noon.

Caribou

The caribou is also known as the reindeer. Unlike other deer species, both males and females have antlers. They feed on lichen in the winter, and grass in the summer, when they migrate to the grasslands of the Arctic tundra.

Both male and female caribou have antlers.

RABBITS, HARES, AND SQUIRRELS

Rabbits and hares are no longer classed as rodents. They are part of the lagomorph family and are found in all areas of the world. They feed mostly on plants, and have particularly sharp teeth called incisors to eat tough stems.

Snowshoe hares have particularly long back feet. Their fur changes from brown in summer to white in winter.

Brown hares are seldom seen during the daytime.

Brown hare

The brown, or European, hare is a very fast runner with long hind legs. It is mostly active at night and spends the day in a shallow dip in the ground known as a form, hidden among vegetation. It eats leaves, bark, roots, berries, and mushrooms.

European rabbit

European rabbits live together in a complex system of burrows called a warren. They eat mainly grass and leafy plants, but they will also do damage to crops and young trees. Female rabbits can have several litters of three to nine young each year.

Rabbit warrens can be home to up to 200 rabbits.

Gray squirrel

The gray squirrel is a rodent. Its natural habitat is the forests of North America. It feeds on seeds and nuts, but will also eat eggs, young birds, and insects. Squirrels will also strip bark from trees to reach the sap beneath.

FANTASTIC FACT

There were no rabbits in Australia until the 18th century. A few were brought into the country but escaped into the wild. Now the population is huge!

Gray squirrels are at home in the country or the town.

47

SHREWS, MICE, AND RATS

Mice and rats belong to the rodent family and include more than 900 species. They are subdivided into those living in North and South America, called New World rodents, and those in Europe, Africa and Asia, called Old World rodents.

The house mouse was bred to become the pet or fancy mouse.

House mouse

Mice eat relatively little, but they can spoil vast quantities of stored food such as grain. Wild mice are only active at night and have keen hearing. They feed on grass seeds and plant stems and, occasionally, insects.

Black rat

Black rats are also known as house or ship rats. They have an extremely varied diet and have adapted to environments around the world. The female rat can have a litter of up to ten young every six weeks or so.

Rats are considered to be dirty, but they spend a lot of time grooming.

The shrew's long nose makes it easy to tell apart from a mouse.

Shrew

Shrews are active at night and are not often seen during the day. They have particularly long noses, and eat mostly invertebrates like earthworms. Shrews have poor eyesight, but do have a very keen sense of smell.

BATS

Bats are small mammals that rest and sleep during the day, and come out at night to feed. Most bats have furry bodies and a pair of leathery wings. They have a special ability called **echolocation** that helps them find their prey using sound.

Bats, along with insects and birds, are the only animals that can truly fly.

Types of bat

Bats are divided into two groups, the megabats and the microbats. Megabats are the fruit bats, also known as flying foxes. These are large bats with big, round eyes. Microbats are mostly smaller, insect-eating bats with small eyes and large ears.

The flying fox is a fruit bat with a face that looks similar to a fox.

Bats prefer to roost in caves that are neither too hot nor too cold.

Living together

When bats are not flying, they roost in a dry place where they are safe from predators. Most bats roost together in a **colony**. As many as 200,000 fruit bats may roost in one tree, and up to 20 million Mexican free-tailed bats can roost in one cave.

Where do bats live?

Bats hang upside-down from trees and the walls of caves. They cannot stand on the ground. Bats can be found in many habitats, from **tropical** rain forests to deserts and grasslands around the world. They have also moved into roofs, lofts, and large barns.

This brown long-eared bat is clinging to a roof with its front and back claws.

BAT FOOD AND BAT FLIGHT

A bat's wings are formed from two layers of skin stretched over its arms and four extra-long fingers stretching down to its legs. As bats fly in the dark, they use sound to help them work out where the objects around them are.

Fruit bats carry fruit away with them in this way to help spread their seeds.

Bat food

Bats must eat a lot of food every day to keep their bodies working properly. Fruit bats eat plant-based food and **nectar** from flowers. The smaller microbats eat insects that they catch while flying, but some bats eat frogs, rats, mice, and even fish.

The leaf-like flap on the nose of a horseshoe bat helps it direct sound

Bat sounds

Humans cannot hear most bat sounds. The high-pitched sounds a bat makes with its mouth or nose bounces off objects, creating echoes that the bat can use to make a picture in its mind of where an object or an insect is. This is called echolocation.

FANTASTIC FACT

A female vampire bat will adopt a young bat that has lost its mother.

Some fruit bats can hover as they sip nectar from flowers.

Vampire bats do not suck blood. Rather, they sip it as it flows from two tiny wounds they make.

Vampire bats

The vampire bat feeds on the blood of other animals when it comes out at night. There are three types of vampire bat and all three live in Central and South America. They feed on the blood of horses, pigs, and cows, but hardly ever people.

GAME BIRDS AND WILDFOWL

Grouse and turkeys belong to a large family of small to large game birds. This family also includes pheasants, quails, and partridges. Geese and ducks belong to the wildfowl family, which also includes swans.

Swans, ducks, and geese all belong to the wildfowl family.

Common turkey

The common turkey is a large bird with bare skin on its head and neck, and spurs on the backs of its legs. Turkeys are strong flyers over short distances. They roost in trees, but find food such as seeds, nuts, berries, and insects on the ground.

The turkey's natural habitat is North American wooded country.

54

Grouse

The grouse's natural habitat is on moorland and in forests across northern Europe and northern Asia. In spring, the males gather in one place. Each day at sunrise, the males call and dance to attract the females.

The male grouse spreads and displays his tail to attract the female.

Canada goose

There are 12 races of Canada goose, divided by region, living anywhere from Arctic tundra to semi-desert areas. They feed by day on grassland vegetation and water plants. They migrate, returning to breed where they were born.

Canadian geese use the same migratory routes from generation to generation.

Mallard

The mallard is the ancestor of all domestic ducks except for Muscovy ducks. Mallards often feed with their tails up in shallow water. They eat many things, including small fish and fish eggs, slugs and worms, water plants, small berries, frogs, and insects.

Only the male mallard has the distinctive green head feathers.

FANTASTIC FACT

Only female ducks quack! Male ducks, or drakes, make a very quiet, rasping noise.

PARROTS AND HUMMINGBIRDS

There are 358 species of parrot, including budgerigars, cockatoos, and macaws. Unlike other bird species, parrots have two toes facing forward and two that face backward. Hummingbirds are named for the noise their fast-moving wings make.

Budgerigar

Pet budgerigars are found in many colors. In the wild, they are mainly green. They are active in the early morning and late afternoon, scratching the ground for seeds, their main food. They are swift and agile when they fly.

Budgerigars live in flocks, from small groups to huge gatherings of birds..

Sulfur-crested cockatoo

Sulfur-crested cockatoos live in Australasia and are noisy, sociable birds. During the breeding season, they live in pairs or family groups, but live in flocks of hundreds of birds for the rest of the year. They feed on seeds, fruit, nuts, insects, and **larvae.**

Sulfur-crested cockatoos can live to the age of 65.

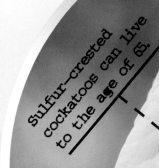

Scarlet macaw

The scarlet macaw is one of the largest and most colorful parrots. Its numbers are declining in the wild because of the destruction of the rainforest, and because young birds are caught to sell as pets. They feed on seeds, nuts, fruit, and berries.

Scarlet macaws live in pairs, in family groups or in flocks of up to 20.

Ruby-throated hummingbird

These tiny birds are only about three inches long, but they breed in south-east Canada and then migrate about 497 miles across the Gulf of Mexico for the winter. They feed on insects and nectar, hovering motionless in front of the flower while feeding.

A hummingbird's wings flap about 80 times per second.

57

HAWKS, KITES, AND BUZZARDS

Most birds of prey are fierce predators that are active during the day. They have sharp eyes, strong feet with claws for seizing prey, and a hooked beak for tearing apart their catch.

FANTASTIC FACT

All sorts of strange things have been found in kite nests, even small childrens' toys!

Birds of prey, like this red kite, soar over open country looking for prey.

Red kite

The red kite is a large bird with long wings and a deeply forked tail. Kites breed in woodland but hunt in open country. They can hover briefly in one spot, and fly with agility. Red kites catch small mammals, birds, reptiles, frogs, fish, and insects.

Common buzzard

The buzzard will prey upon small mammals, reptiles, insects, and some ground birds. It catches its prey by dropping onto it from its perch or from hovering flight. The male buzzard courts the female by performing spectacular dives and swoops in the air.

Common buzzards are found in Europe, Asia, and East Africa.

The red-tailed hawk's habitat ranges from deserts to forests and mountains.

Red-tailed hawk

The powerful red-tailed hawk is an aggressive bird with a loud voice and a vivid chestnut-colored tail. It eats mostly small mammals, but will also eat snakes, lizards, birds, and insects. It hunts when flying or swoops down from a perch.

FALCONS, KESTRELS, AND OSPREYS

The falcon family includes birds such as kestrels as well as falcons. The peregrine falcon is the fastest flyer of all birds. Falcons can be found all over the world. The osprey is the only species in its family.

FANTASTIC FACT
Peregrine falcons can dive at speeds of up to 200 miles per hour!

Peregrine falcon

The peregrine falcon is almost unequalled in speed and precision of flight. Its chief prey is pigeons, doves, and starlings, which it can chase and capture in mid-air.

Peregrine falcons make a dramatic high-speed dive straight down onto prey.

Osprey

The osprey is also known as the fish hawk. It feeds mostly on fish, but it will sometimes also take small mammals and wounded birds. When hunting, it flies over water, hovering briefly before plunging feet-first into the water.

Ospreys will fly with their catch facing head-first, to ease any wind resistance.

Common kestrel

Kestrels hunt over open ground. They hover and watch some 33 to 49 feet above the ground, and once the prey is spotted, drop gently down onto it. Kestrels mostly eat small mammals, but they will also eat small birds, reptiles, and insects.

Kestrels can hover for several minutes, keeping their heads perfectly still

EAGLES

Eagles are among the largest and most powerful of all birds. They are birds of prey, hunting other animals for food. To help them hunt, eagles have powerful hooked beaks, excellent eyesight, and feet ending in sharp, curved talons.

The name "bald eagle" is from the Old English word "balde", meaning white.

Eagle types

There are about 60 different species of eagle. Most eagles are larger and more powerful than other birds of prey, such as hawks. Eagles are divided into four groups: snake eagles, fish and sea eagles, booted eagles, and giant forest eagles.

Eagles have a fierce-looking ridge over their eyes, as on this monkey-eating eagle.

Where can you find eagles?

Eagles live in almost every kind of habitat, from deserts and forests to coasts and farmland. Bald eagles and golden eagles are found in the USA and Canada. Harpy eagles live in the South American rainforest. Martial eagles live in the South African savanna.

Four eagle groups

Snake eagles are smaller and feed on snakes. Bald eagles belong to the fish and sea eagle group. Booted eagles have thickly feathered legs. The huge and powerful giant forest eagles live in tropical rainforest.

The greater spotted eagle is a member of the booted eagle group.

FANTASTIC FACT

Snake eagles have thick scales on their legs to protect them from snake bites. They attack snakes up to ten feet long!

EAGLE SENSES AND SKILLS

Eagles can see at least four times better than a human can. An eagle can spot a rabbit one mile away. Their hearing is very sharp, so they can hear the noises made by their prey, but their sense of smell is poor.

Hunting

Eagles hunt during the day to make the most of their excellent sight. Some stay perfectly still on a tree or ledge so their prey does not notice them, then dive down and grab it. Other eagles, like the golden eagle, fly around looking for prey.

An eagle's eyes cannot move sideways. It has to turn its whole head to look around.

The eagle uses its powerful hooked talons to catch and carry prey.

Building a nest

Eagles build huge nests in places that are difficult to reach. Eagle nests are also called eyries, and are made from twigs. Eagles return to the same nest every year. Many eagles mate for life, living with the same partner until one dies.

Young eagles usually inherit different colored feathers from their parents.

FANTASTIC FACT

A group of several eagles soaring together in a thermal is called a "kettle of eagles".

The eagle's wing feathers are separated at the tips, to make flight smoother.

Soaring through the air

Eagles are experts at flying. Their wings are ideally shaped for gliding. They can stay in the air for hours and hardly have to flap their wings at all. Eagles fly high in the sky using **thermals**, currents of warm air rising from the ground.

OWLS

Many people have heard an owl hooting at night, but it is unusual to see an owl in the wild. Owls are closely related to birds of prey such as eagles and falcons. There are about 200 species of owl, divided into two groups: barn owls and true owls.

Barn owls

Barn owls have a heart-shaped face and long legs, with mostly pale feathers. Barn owls have a special claw on their middle toes, which they use to comb their feathers.

The barn owl is one of the best-known owls in the world.

FANTASTIC FACT
The largest-ever owl lived several million years ago. It was more than three feet tall!

True owls

True owls vary in size. They have a big head with large, round eyes and a round face. Some have tufts of feathers at the tips of their ears. Their legs are covered in feathers and their innermost toes are shorter than the middle toes.

This scops owl hunts at night and sits in trees during the day.

Snowy owls are found mainly in the Arctic.

Where do owls live?

Owls are found in all parts of the world except Antarctica and parts of Greenland. Snowy owls are found in icy tundra in the far north, and the tiny elf owl lives in the hot deserts of North America. Most owls prefer woodland and forests.

OWL SENSES AND SKILLS

Owls have very sharp eyes and can see in poor light. They cannot move their eyes, so they must swivel their heads instead. They also have good hearing and can hunt in total darkness, using sound to find and catch their prey.

This Short-eared owl relies on its hearing to hunt voles.

Owl hearing

The feathers on an owl's face funnel sounds towards its ears. In barn owls, one ear is slightly higher than the other, so that sounds do not reach them at exactly the same time. By turning their heads, they can locate the source of the sound very accurately.

A Saw-whet owl swooping down to catch its prey in its talons.

Flying

Most birds make a flapping noise when they fly. Owls' wings are different. They have soft feathers at the front edge of their wings that let them swoop down silently on their prey. They can fly at speed, but can also slow their flight while they are hunting.

FANTASTIC FACT

The Short-eared owl may fly up to 1,247 miles between its winter and summer homes!

Feeding

Owls are carnivores. They feed on animals such as insects, birds, and small mammals, including voles, mice, and rabbits. Owls swallow their food whole, including bones, fur, and feathers. Later, they will cough up the indigestible parts as a pellet.

PENGUINS

Penguins are easy to recognize, with their black backs and white fronts. They are plump, with short legs and webbed feet. Penguin cannot fly, but they are excellent swimmers. They stand very upright on their back legs and waddle when they walk.

Penguin types

There are 17 species of penguin. The largest are the Emperor and King penguins. The King penguin has an orange teardrop on the side of its head, but the Emperor penguin's markings are yellow. The chicks' feathers are also very different.

Crested penguins

Six species of penguins have a crest of feathers on their heads. These crested birds are called Erect-crested, Fiordland, Macaroni, Rockhopper, Royal, and Snares penguins.

King penguins have orange markings on their head and neck.

The macaroni penguin has a vivid crest of yellow feathers on its head.

Other penguin types

There are eight other species of penguin. They are the Adélie, African, Chinstrap, Galapagos, Gentoo, Humboldt, Magellanic and Yellow-eyed penguins.

The Chinstrap penguin is named after the thin black line running under its chin.

FANTASTIC FACT

Galapagos penguins shade their feet in summer so they do not get sunburned!

Where do penguins live?

There are no penguins in the Arctic. Only two species of penguin, the Adélie and the Emperor, live in the Antarctic all year round. Most species only visit Antarctica in the summer. They live along the coasts of the cold Southern Ocean.

PENGUIN FAMILY LIFE

Penguins like to be close to other penguins. When they are on land, they live in large groups called colonies that can have 400 or 40,000 penguins in them! Each mated pair of penguins has its own space in the colony where they make their nest.

Laying eggs

Penguins come onto land to mate and to breed. Most penguins make a simple nest of feathers, grass, or even small rocks. Only one or two eggs are laid, and they are kept warm by both parents, taking it in turns to look after the eggs.

Emperor and King penguins keep their eggs warm under a fold of skin.

Emperor penguin eggs

In the middle of winter, Emperor penguins walk inland to their breeding site, or rookery. They build no nest. The male places the female's egg on his feet and covers it with a flap of skin to keep it warm. The female Emperor penguin returns to the sea for two months to feed, leaving the male to **incubate** the egg.

FANTASTIC FACT

The Emperor penguin can dive down to 1,738 feet to catch fish, staying underwater for 20 minutes!

Older penguin chicks are left in groups called creches while their parents feed.

Keeping warm

Male Emperor penguins huddle together, shuffling forward all the time, taking turns to walk to the edge of the huddle where it is coldest. The males do not eat while incubating an egg, and can lose up to 45 percent of their body weight.

Young chicks stay warm under a fold of skin. They are kept off the ice by their parents' feet.

Hatching

Two months after the egg is laid, the Emperor penguin chick hatches. The male penguin brings up a meal from his stomach to feed it, then the female penguin returns from the sea and takes over. The male walks slowly back to the sea to feed.

SWIMMING AND FISHING

The penguin's body is streamlined to move through the water easily. They use their wings like flippers to push them through the water. Their webbed feet act like paddles when on the surface or for steering when underwater.

These brown, fluffy King penguin chicks look very unlike their parents.

Penguin plumage

Penguin chicks have fluffy feathers that trap heat and help keep them warm. These fluffy feathers are not waterproof, so penguin chicks cannot go into the water until they have adult feathers. The adult feathers are waterproof.

74

In the water and on land

Once young penguins have their waterproof adult feathers, they can learn to swim. At first they return to land each night, but soon they spend most of their time at sea. On land, they look clumsy, but their waddle saves energy and keeps them warm.

Penguin food

Penguins mostly eat fish, squid, and **krill**. Each penguin species has a beak shaped to catch prey. King penguins have a long, curved beak to catch large squid. The Humboldt penguin has a short, thick beak for catching small fish.

Penguins leap from the ice into the water.

Penguins swing one leg forward and then the other, rocking from side to side.

Many penguins feed on krill, tiny shrimp—like crustaceans.

75

SPARROWS AND FINCHES

There are 36 species of sparrow, found in Africa and Eurasia to Indonesia. The European sparrows, known as Old World sparrows, are a separate species from the New World sparrows. Finches are a widely distributed group of small seed-eating songbirds.

The male cardinal is unmistakable, with brilliant red plumage.

Northern cardinal

Northern cardinals are aggressive and territorial birds with a varied range of songs. They are found mainly in Canada and the USA. Cardinals feed on the ground and in trees, and eat seeds and berries. They also take insects in the breeding season.

Blue-gray tanager

The blue-gray tanager is found in both humid and dry areas, in coastal lowlands and up to a height of 7217 feet. They forage in pairs or in small flocks for berries, fruit, and insects, which they catch on the wing or take from leaves.

The blue-gray tanager is a medium-sized South American songbird.

Purple honeycreeper

The purple honeycreeper lives in wooded areas in northern South America. Fruit, especially bananas, and insects are its main foods. These birds will also perch beside flowers and suck nectar from them with their long, curved bills.

The purple honeycreeper is a member of the tanager family.

FANTASTIC FACT

In spite of their name, female purple honeycreepers are green!

Chipping sparrows live in open woodland, gardens, and parks.

Chipping sparrow

This New World sparrow is found across Canada, USA, Mexico, Central America, and Nicaragua. They often live in suburban and inhabited areas. Their main food is grass seed, but they also eat weed seeds, insects, and spiders.

TORTOISES AND TURTLES

Tortoises and turtles are reptiles, and are cold-blooded animals. They first appeared more than 200 million years ago, when the dinosaurs were still on Earth. They have changed very little in all this time, and are easily identified by their shells.

Types of tortoise and turtle

There are about 290 species of tortoise and turtle, and all of them have a shell. There are 60 bones in the shell, which is covered by large plates for extra protection. Tortoise shells are domed. Turtle shells are flatter, to move through the water easily.

This giant tortoise has a heavy, domed shell and thick legs.

Hiding in shells

Tortoises and turtles can be divided into two groups: the hidden-necked and the side-necked. Hidden-necked turtles and tortoises pull their heads straight into their shells. Side-necked turtles pull their heads in sideways under the edge of their shells.

Tortoises pull their heads into their shells when threatened by predators

These painted turtles are warming their bodies in the sun.

FANTASTIC FACT

The giant leatherback turtle's shell can be nearly eight feet long!

Where do tortoises and turtles live?

Tortoises and turtles are found on every continent except Antarctica. Tortoises and freshwater turtles are found in tropical and subtropical climates. Sea turtles are found mostly in tropical oceans, but some swim north—almost to the Arctic.

79

TRAVELING TORTOISES AND TURTLES

Tortoises are well known for their slow walk, but turtles can swim surprisingly quickly and can catch prey. Tortoises eat mostly leaves and fruit. Sea turtles eat a variety of animals, including jellyfish, corals, sea urchins, crabs, and fish.

FANTASTIC FACT

Desert tortoises store water inside their bodies. They use it when they cannot find drinking water.

The Texas tortoise lives alone in dry, sandy areas of Texas and Mexico.

On land

Tortoises have large feet with short toes. They need sturdy feet to lift their bodies and heavy shells off the ground. Tortoises each have an area they stay within, or territory. Unlike most other animals, they do not defend their space, so tortoise territories can overlap.

In the water

Freshwater turtles must be able to walk on land and swim in fresh water. They generally live in shallow lakes or rivers. Sea turtles do not have to come to the surface to breathe, because they can take in oxygen from the water through the skin and throat.

Sea turtles can stay underwater for weeks at a time.

Laying eggs

Turtles and tortoises lay leathery eggs in a dug-out hole, and then cover them up again. Female sea turtles return to the beach on which they were born every year or so to lay their own eggs. Scientists are unsure how the turtles find their way back.

Turtles, such as this hawksbill, navigate their way across huge oceans.

CROCODILES AND ALLIGATORS

Crocodiles and alligators are fierce predators that live near water. They are the largest of Earth's reptiles, which are animals that have a skin covered with dry **scales**. Most reptiles, including crocodiles and alligators, lay eggs with a leathery shell.

Both crocodiles and alligators, like this American alligator, have powerful jaws.

Gharials have very long, thin snouts with a pot-like tip.

Types of crocodile

There are 23 different species of crocodile and alligator, divided into three families: alligators, crocodiles, and gharials. The alligator family also includes caimans. The crocodile family includes saltwater, Nile, New Guinea and American crocodiles.

Telling them apart

The large fourth tooth in the lower jaw of an alligator is not visible when the alligator's mouth is closed. In crocodiles, this tooth can be seen even when the crocodile's mouth is shut.

A crocodile's large fourth tooth is visible even when its mouth is shut.

Where do you find crocodiles and alligators?

Crocodiles and alligators live mostly in the tropical and subtropical parts of the world, around the Equator. Alligators are found only in south-eastern USA and in China. Caimans live mostly in Central and South America. Crocodiles are more widespread.

What do crocodiles and alligators eat?

Crocodiles and alligators feed on a wide range of animals. They have powerful jaws with which they crush the bodies of their prey. Usually the prey drowns as the crocodile or alligator dives underwater with its catch.

FANTASTIC FACT

Alligators have between 74 and 80 teeth. As the teeth wear down, they are replaced.

CROCODILE AND ALLIGATOR LIFE

Crocodiles and alligators are carnivorous reptiles. They are cold-blooded, unlike mammals. The females lay between 10 and 50 leathery eggs in a nest, which they guard, and do not leave except to cool off in the shade.

Female crocodiles and alligators look after their young carefully.

Hatchling care

Female crocodiles and alligators look after their babies, or hatchlings, for several months. Young American alligators will stay close to their mothers for up to two years. The young adults will then move out into the surrounding area.

These Nile crocodiles are guarding their eggs.

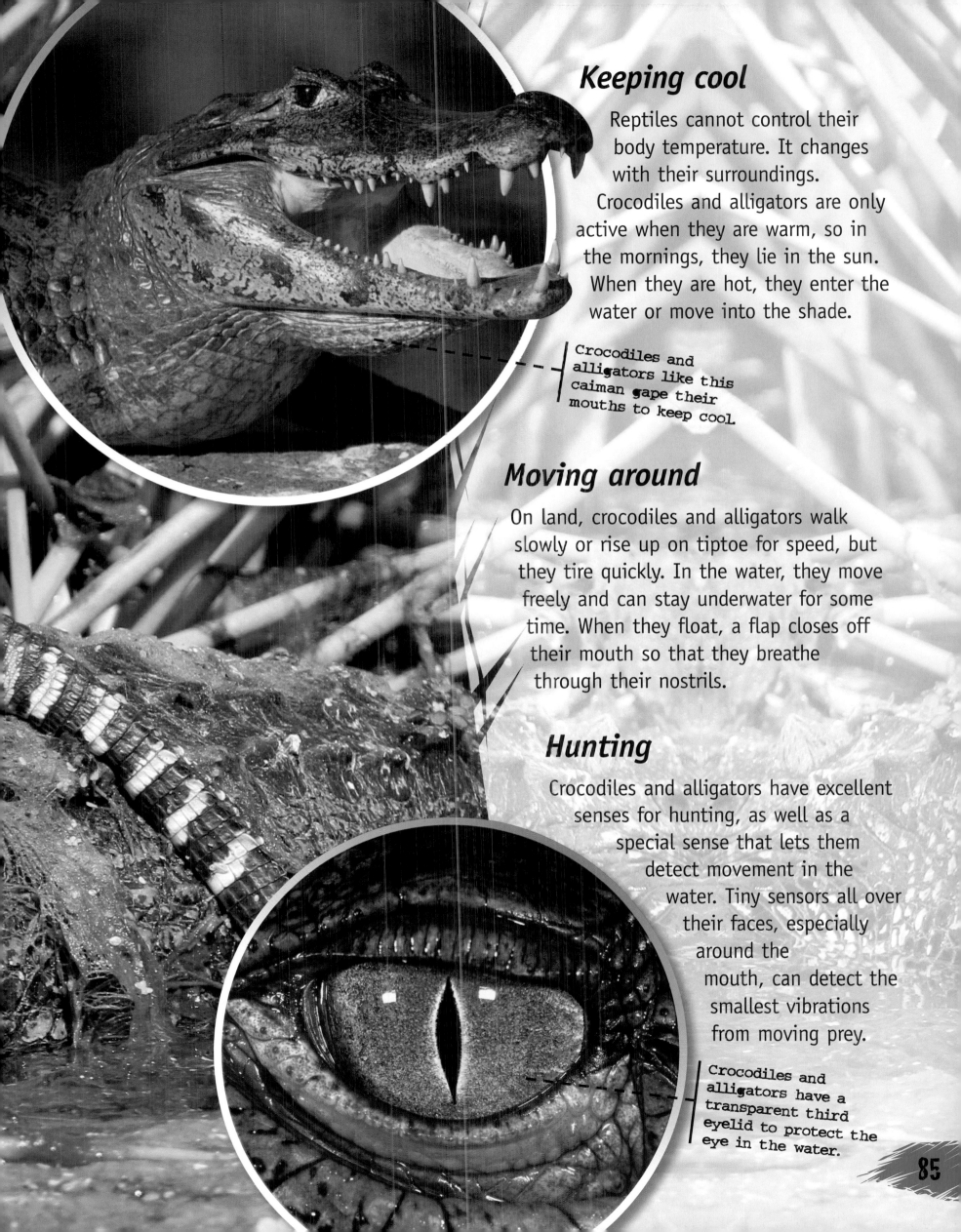

Keeping cool

Reptiles cannot control their body temperature. It changes with their surroundings.

Crocodiles and alligators are only active when they are warm, so in the mornings, they lie in the sun. When they are hot, they enter the water or move into the shade.

Crocodiles and alligators like this caiman gape their mouths to keep cool

Moving around

On land, crocodiles and alligators walk slowly or rise up on tiptoe for speed, but they tire quickly. In the water, they move freely and can stay underwater for some time. When they float, a flap closes off their mouth so that they breathe through their nostrils.

Hunting

Crocodiles and alligators have excellent senses for hunting, as well as a special sense that lets them detect movement in the water. Tiny sensors all over their faces, especially around the mouth, can detect the smallest vibrations from moving prey.

Crocodiles and alligators have a transparent third eyelid to protect the eye in the water.

TYPES OF SNAKES

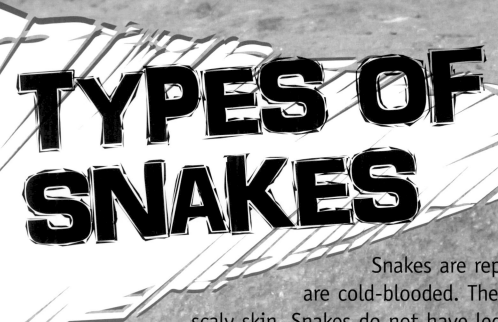

Snakes are reptiles and are cold-blooded. They have scaly skin. Snakes do not have legs, but they do have a very long, flexible backbone. This allows them to bend in any direction, raise their heads, and even tie themselves into coils and knots.

Types of snake

There are almost 3,000 species of snake, ranging in size from five-inch garter snakes to nearly 11-yard boas and pythons. Most snakes are between about ten inches and nearly five feet long. Snakes usually blend in with their surroundings, but poisonous snakes are brightly colored.

A rattlesnake's rattle is caused by sections of dried skin knocking together.

The red, yellow and black stripes of this coral snake warn others that it is very poisonous.

How do snakes move?

Most snakes live on land. They burrow into sand and under rocks, and some live in trees. They slither along the ground, moving from side to side in a series of curves. Sea snakes have flattened tails, which they use like a paddle.

Where do snakes live?

Snakes are usually found in warmer areas. They do not live near the North and South Poles, as it is far too cold for them. Many islands, including Iceland, Ireland, and New Zealand, do not have snakes either. Sea snakes live in the world's warmer seas.

The sea krait is beautiful, but it is also deadly.

HUNTING AND DEFENSE

Snakes cannot see very well, but they have excellent hearing and a very good sense of smell. They taste the air with their forked tongues through a slot in their upper jaw and a special sense organ on the roof of the mouth.

Pit vipers and pythons have heat-sensitive pits on their snouts for hunting at night.

FANTASTIC FACT

The largest snakes can survive on only one really good meal a year!

Hunting

Snakes are predators. Many snakes hunt a range of animals, from insects and worms to lizards and mice. Huge snakes like boa constrictors and pythons can swallow deer, goats, and even people. Snakes' teeth face backward to stop their prey from escaping.

The Gabon viper hides in fallen leaves while it waits to ambush prey.

Catching and eating prey

Heavy snakes hunt by moving in a straight line. The scales underneath their body hook onto the ground, pulling it forward. Snakes swallow their prey whole. They can open their mouths very wide, because their lower jaw is loosely joined to their skull.

Poisonous snakes

Many snakes produce **venom** to kill their prey and for protection. A snake's venom is produced in a gland in its head. The venom is pumped into its prey through a long, sharp tooth called a fang. Some venom kills quickly, other venom just weakens prey.

This sedge viper is ready to attack, and is showing the fangs on its upper jaw.

Constrictors

Many of the largest snakes, like boas and pythons, are constrictors. They squeeze their prey by coiling their bodies around it and tightening the coils until it cannot breathe. Once the prey is dead, the snake uncoils slightly and swallows the prey head-first.

89

LIZARDS

There are over 3,000 species of lizard. They live in many habitats: in trees, on the ground, and in the water. Lizards include iguanas and chameleons. There are more than 600 species in the iguana family. About 85 species of chameleon are known.

Common iguana

The common iguana has a crest of comb-like spines running all the way down its body and tail. The bands across the body become darker with age. Young iguanas are bright green. Iguanas are agile plant-eaters, and are active during the day.

Common or green iguanas are popular pets, but they need special care.

FANTASTIC FACT

A chameleon's tongue strikes its prey in one teenth of the speed of a blink.

Frilled lizard

The slender, long-tailed frilled lizard has an extraordinary collar of skin around its shoulders. Normally this collar lies in folds around its neck, but if alarmed, the lizard opens its mouth wide and lifts its frill, making the animal look larger than it really is.

The frilled lizard is found in northern Australia and New Guinea.

Jackson's chameleon

The male Jackson's chameleon has three horns on its head. Chameleons change their skin color to reflect their emotional state. Chameleons have very long tongues, which they extend to catch their prey. They can rotate and focus each eye separately.

Jackson's chameleons are colored to look like lichen on the bark of a tree.

FANTASTIC FACT

A chameleon's tongue hits its prey in about 30 thousandths of a second -- one-tenth the speed of a blink!

FROGS AND TOADS

Frogs and toads live both on land and in water. Most frogs have smooth, moist skin, and long back legs for leaping. Toads have drier, more bumpy skin and shorter back legs for crawling. Frogs and toads catch their prey using a long, sticky tongue.

Glass frogs have see-through skin, which means you can see inside their bodies.

Frog and toad types

Frogs and toads are amphibians. There are more than 4,500 different types of frog and toad in the world. These are divided into 28 families.

Tree frogs have sticky pads on their fingers and toes to grip leaves and twigs.

Tree frogs

Tree frogs have slender bodies and long legs, with sticky pads on their fingers and toes that help them cling to branches. They are active at night.

Clawed frogs

Clawed frogs spend their whole life in water. They put food into their mouths with their fingers. This is because they have no tongues, unlike other frogs and toads.

Where do you find frogs and toads?

Frogs and toads live in all the world's continents except the Antarctic. Most live near fresh water. Frogs and toads can survive in many different climates, from the desert to the rain forest, and even cope with extreme cold.

Lumpy toads

Many toads, such as the common toad, have two lumps just behind their eyes. These ooze a foul liquid when the toad is attacked.

A common toad oozes toxins when threatened by a snake.

FROM TADPOLES TO FROGS AND TOADS

Frogs and toads lay eggs in clumps or chains, surrounded by a coat of protective jelly. The common frog's eggs are called frogspawn. The eggs hatch into tadpoles, which live in the water as they change into frogs or toads.

The back legs of the tadpole of a common frog appear after eight weeks.

The tadpole embryos of these common frogs can be seen inside the adult frog's eggs.

Tadpoles

Tadpole embryos develop a head, tail, and feathery **gills**. When a tadpole hatches, it uses the gills to breathe underwater. After a while, these disappear and are replaced by gills inside its body. Later, the tadpole grows two back legs, then two front legs.

Feeding

When they first hatch, tadpoles feed on plants and algae in the water. After they become older, they catch and eat small insects. Adult frogs and toads have large mouths. Once their prey is inside, small backward-facing teeth stop it from escaping.

This young frog, or froglet, now has lungs but still has what is left of its tail

Moving on to land

A tadpole's body changes further as it becomes a young frog or toad. Gradually, it grows slimmer, its tail shortens and finally disappears, its mouth widens, and its eyes get rounder and bulge out. Its gills are replaced by lungs that can breathe air.

SALAMANDERS

Salamanders are lizard-like, tailed amphibians that live both on land and in water. Around 350 species of salamander are known, 250 of which are lungless salamanders. These take in oxygen through their skins as they do not have lungs.

The tiger salamander is in a group of 32 species called mole salamanders.

Tiger salamander

This is the world's largest land-dwelling salamander. It has a stout body, broad head, and small eyes. Tiger salamanders vary greatly in color, and are found in a variety of low-lying and high-altitude habitats. They eat mostly worms, insects, and mice.

Red salamander

The red salamander is brilliantly colored, with a stout, long body and short tail and legs. It spends much of its life on land and usually lives close to water. It eats mostly earthworms, insects, and smaller salamanders.

The axolotl keeps features of its larval form, such as feathery external gills.

The red salamander is found in eastern USA, in Indiana and Louisiana.

Axolotl

Now rare, axolotls are in danger from the loss of their habitat in Mexico. Living in water at high altitudes, axolotls can spend most of their life in a larval form. They even breed in this form. However if their pond dries out, they may mature into a salamander.

FANTASTIC FACT

If an axolotl is injured and loses one of its legs or its tail, it can regrow a new one!

NEWTS AND CAECILIANS

Newts are a type of salamander. They have well-developed legs with four or five toes. Adult newts have lungs instead of external gills. Newts are found both on land and in water. Caecilians are amphibians without legs, like giant earthworms.

Male great crested newts are often smaller than females, but females have no crest.

Great crested newt

Also called the warty newt, this large newt is found in northern Europe. The male has a jagged crest on his back during the breeding season. Great crested newts eat mostly invertebrates, but they will also eat small fish and other amphibians and their eggs.

Sticky caecilian

Adult sticky caecilians live in burrows in south-east Asia. They feed on earthworms and small burrowing snakes. The female lays about 20 eggs in burrows in moist ground. She coils around the eggs, which absorb moisture and double in size.

The sticky caecilian is found in forest habitats.

FANTASTIC FACT

The largest hellbender that has been recorded was over 2.5 feet long!

Hellbender

Despite its name, this giant salamander is a harmless creature that feeds on crayfish, snails and worms. The hellbender has fully developed lungs. It is active at night and depends on its sense of smell and touch, rather than sight, to catch its prey.

Hellbenders do not have teeth; they have hard, bony mouths in their place.

99

SHARKS

Sharks have a backbone. Their skeletons are made of cartilage. They have a large, triangular dorsal fin on the tops of their backs, and large pectoral fins behind their gill slits, which help with balance. Sharks must keep swimming or they will sink.

This blue shark has five gill slits on either side of its head

Types of shark

There are more than 360 species of shark, divided into 30 families. Some are as small as your hand, while others are larger than a bus. More than half of all sharks are under 35 inches long. The largest sharks are found out in the open seas and oceans.

Tiger sharks can be up to 20 feet long.

Swimming

Most sharks have to carry on swimming all the time, to keep water moving over their gills; otherwise they cannot breathe. If they stop swimming, they will sink. Most fish have an organ called a swim bladder to stop them from sinking. Sharks do not have this.

Most sharks do not sleep, but, like this horn shark, they can rest.

FANTASTIC FACT

A shark's pectoral fins cannot bend upward like other fish, so sharks cannot swim backward.

Baby sharks

Most sharks give birth to live young. Baby sharks are called pups and look like miniature adult sharks. Some sharks, like dogfish sharks, lay eggs outside their bodies. These are protected by a tough case that attaches itself to rocks or seaweed.

Some sharks lay eggs in tough cases. These are called "mermaid's purses."

SHARKS AS PREDATORS

Sharks eat a variety of prey, but their main food is fish and invertebrates such as squid and octopus. The larger sharks can catch bigger prey, including turtles, seals, and even dolphins. Other sharks eat crabs, starfish, sea anemones, and sea urchins.

FANTASTIC FACT

Some types of shark get through as many as 30,000 teeth during their lifetimes!

Only the front row of teeth is used by a shark when feeding. The rest are there to replace lost ones.

Shark teeth

A shark's teeth are adapted to the kind of food it eats, and grow bigger as it grows older. Flat teeth are ideal for cruching snails, crabs, and sea urchins, while jagged teeth are better for tearing apart larger animals. Shark pups are born with a full set of teeth.

Some sharks hunt in groups, herding shoals of fish into shallow water.

Hunting

Many sharks attack their prey from below. The shark lurks in deep water, and when it spots its prey, it races after it at great speed, charging upward. Most sharks hunt alone, but species like the sand tiger shark hunt in groups to attack shoals of fish.

Sharks without teeth

Not all sharks are predators. The whale shark and the giant basking shark are filter feeders, eating tiny plants and animals, called **plankton**. They have no teeth and swim with their huge mouths wide open, filtering the sea water through their gills.

Filter feeders, like this whale shark, have huge mouths and enormous gill slits.

RAYS

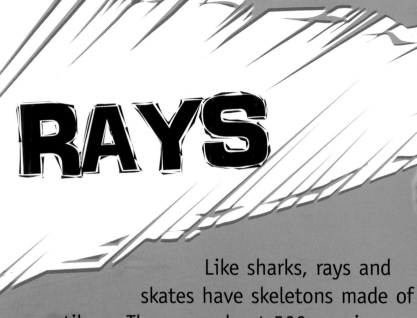

Like sharks, rays and skates have skeletons made of cartilage. There are about 500 species worldwide and most live in the oceans in temperate and tropical waters.

Body shape

Almost all rays and skates have a broad, flat body and very wide pectoral fins, which give the fish a diamond shape. The fins extend the length of the body and meet the whiplike tail. The gill openings and slit-like mouth are on the underside of the body.

Atlantic manta

The Atlantic manta is also known as the giant devil ray, and can be up to 22 feet wide. It has two fleshy projections at each side of its mouth that act as food scoops. Mantas feed on plankton, filtering food out of water with their gills.

Atlantic mantas have special scoops either side of their mouths.

The Atlantic manta ray is the largest species of the ray family.

Southern stingray

Stingrays are almost rectangular and have long, thin tails. They have a venomous spine near the base of the tail that can inflict a serious, sometimes fatal, wound. Stingrays live buried in sand on the sea bed, and eat fish, crustaceans, and molluscs.

Southern stingrays are found off the Atlantic coast and the Gulf of Mexico.

The long saw-shaped snout of the sawfish is called a rostrum.

Smalltooth sawfish

Sawfish are members of the ray and skate family, but they do not have a diamond-shaped body. Sawfish move their long saw-shaped snouts back and forth to saw prey in half or to dig through the sediment on the sea floor. They eat fish and crustaceans.

EELS

Eels belong to the fish family. There are more than 730 species of eel, grouped into about 15 families. Eels can be found in both fresh and sea water worldwide, except in polar regions. All eels have long, slender bodies.

Morays lurk in rocky crevices, showing only their heads, waiting for prey.

Conger eel

The large conger eel is fairly common on rocky shores in the North Atlantic. It has a long body without scales, and its upper jaw overlaps its lower one. Conger eels feed on fish, crustaceans, and octopus.

Conger eels migrate from shallow shores to deeper water to mate.

Moray eel

There are 100 species of moray. Morays are found in tropical and warm temperate oceans. They are without scales and are patterned for camouflage. Morays have a large mouth with strong, sharp teeth, and feed on fish, squid and cuttlefish.

European eels are dark grey in fresh water, and turn silvery in the ocean.

European eel

The European eel is the only eel-like fish to live in fresh water. Young eels or elvers migrate from their freshwater homes to the mid-Atlantic, where they spawn and die. Larval eels are transparent until they migrate back to fresh water, and become elvers.

WHALES

Whales are not fish. They are mammals—animals that produce milk for their young. Whales live in the water but still breathe air. All mammals have some hair, but whales have just a few bristles. A thick layer of blubber keeps whales warm.

The blue whale is the largest animal that has ever lived on the Earth.

The humpback whale swallows great mouthfuls of water as it surfaces.

Whale types

There are about 50 species of whale, divided into two groups called baleen whales and toothed whales. Baleen whales include humpback whales, gray whales, and fin whales. They have huge plates instead of teeth for filtering food from the water.

Toothed whales

Toothed whales include sperm whales, pilot whales, narwhals, and orcas (killer whales). They are smaller than baleen whales and have no plates in their mouths. Toothed whales are predators, hunting fish, squid, and seals.

Toothed whales, like this beluga, have small teeth with which to grip their prey.

Where do whales live?

Whales are found in all the oceans of the world, including the cold Southern and Arctic Oceans. Cold water is rich in food for whales, especially krill and plankton. Since fish eat plankton too, there is food here for both baleen and toothed whales.

WHALE LIFE UNDERWATER

Whales must swim to the surface to breathe air, rather than taking oxygen from the water. They do not breathe through their mouths, but via a large nostril called a **blowhole** on top of their head, which covers a flap just before they dive again.

When whales surface, they breathe out a jet of air and water from the blowhole.

Whale calves like this orca stay close to their mothers.

Whale calves

As soon as a whale calf is born, its mother pushes it to the surface for its first breath of air. The female whale feeds her calf on milk that is rich in fat, and it grows quickly. The calf must learn how to swim, and how to breathe without swallowing water.

FANTASTIC FACT

The blue whale's moans register 80 decibels. This is much louder than a jet engine!

Whale senses

Whales have small eyes and cannot see well. Most whales live in deep, murky water, and cannot see more than three feet away. Their hearing is incredibly sensitive. They have a tiny openings both sides of their heads which lead to internal ears.

Locating prey

Toothed whales use echolocation to find their prey. They send out high-pitched clicks that bounce off objects and return to the whale as an echo. The whale uses the echoes to build a picture of its surroundings, and of the shape and whereabouts of its prey.

Communication

Whales communicate in many ways. They squeak, whistle, moan, and squeal, and these sounds travel great distances underwater. Whales also slap their tails on the surface and leap out of the water to communicate. Humpback whales even sing!

This whale is about to slap its tail on the surface of the water.

iii

DOLPHINS AND PORPOISES

Dolphins and porpoises are intelligent mammals that live in the world's seas and rivers. They do not have gills to take oxygen from the water, like fish. Instead, they have lungs and need to come to the surface to breathe air.

Dolphin and porpoise types

There are 37 species of dolphin and six porpoise species. All porpoises live in the sea, while five species of dolphin live in rivers. Dolphins and porpoises look very similar, but dolphins have sharp, cone-shaped teeth, while porpoise teeth are spade-shaped.

The small spinner dolphin lives mainly in tropical waters.

Dolphins have as many as 90 small, cone-shaped teeth.

Where do dolphins and porpoises live?

Dolphins and porpoises live in all of the world's oceans and seas, even in the Arctic. The common and bottlenose dolphins are found all around the world. River dolphins are found in many large rivers, including the Amazon in South America.

River dolphins have a long, slender beak, a bulging forehead, and a neck.

FANTASTIC FACT

When dolphins open their eyes underwater, special greasy tears protect their eyes from the salt.

The blowhole is a single large nostril on the top of the dolphin's head.

Mammals in water

Dolphins must surface to breathe every couple of minutes, letting out the air through their blowhole to blow away water so they do not get water in their lungs. Dolphins have a thick layer of blubber to keep their body at 96.8 degrees Fahrenheit, almost as warm as a human.

DOLPHIN AND PORPOISE LIFE

Dolphins and porpoises live in large groups known as pods. Most pods have about 10 animals, but the biggest pods have many thousands of dolphins or porpoises in them. Pods hunt together in groups and communicate by whistling.

The torpedo shape of the dolphin and porpoise helps them move rapidly through water.

The bulging forehead of a dolphin or porpoise contains the melon.

Dolphin senses

Dolphins and porpoises have good eyesight. They also use a special sense called echolocation. The **melon** in their bulging foreheads produces whistles and clicks, sounds whose returning echoes help them form a picture of where their prey is.

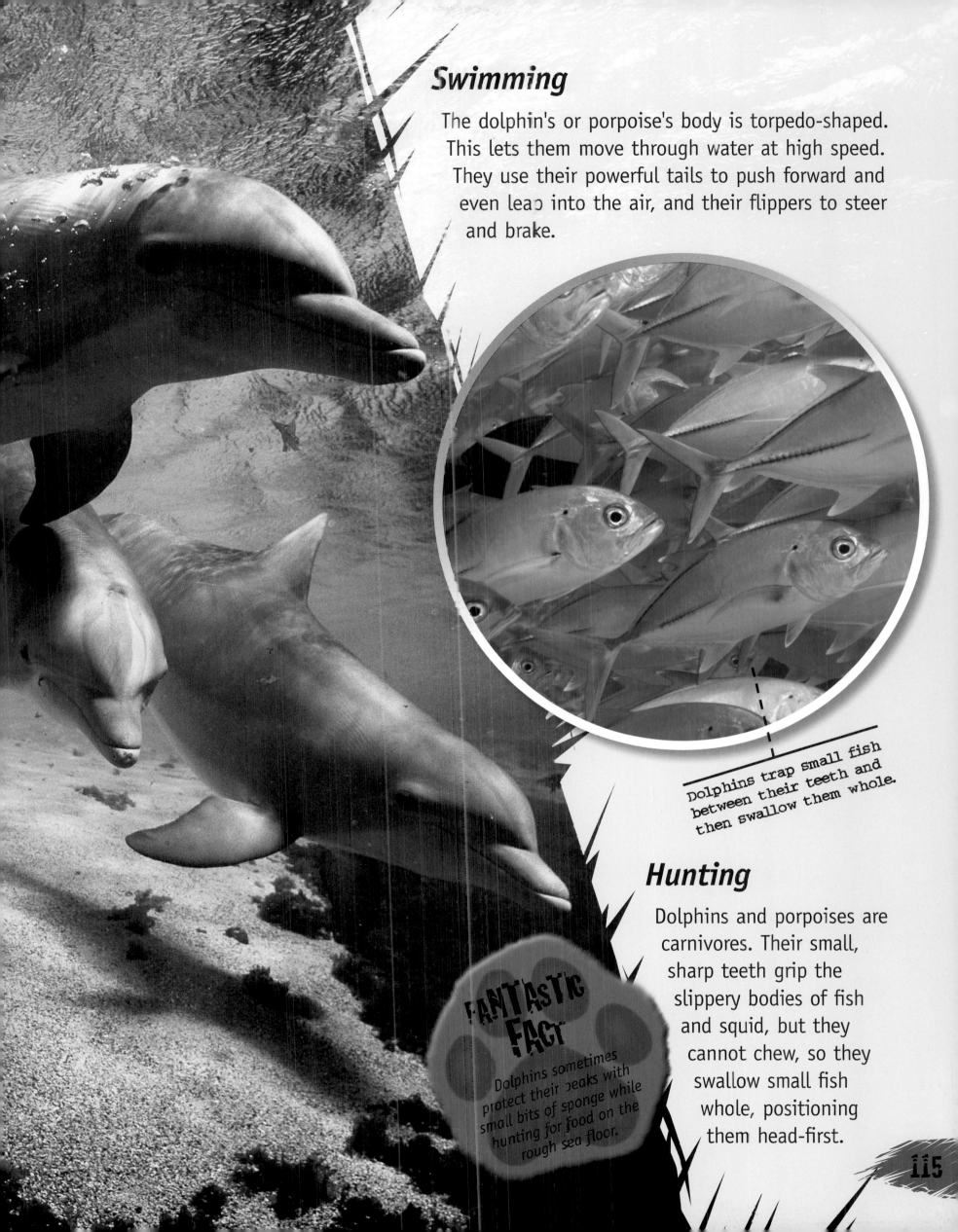

Swimming

The dolphin's or porpoise's body is torpedo-shaped. This lets them move through water at high speed. They use their powerful tails to push forward and even leap into the air, and their flippers to steer and brake.

Dolphins trap small fish between their teeth and then swallow them whole.

Hunting

Dolphins and porpoises are carnivores. Their small, sharp teeth grip the slippery bodies of fish and squid, but they cannot chew, so they swallow small fish whole, positioning them head-first.

FANTASTIC FACT

Dolphins sometimes protect their beaks with small bits of sponge while hunting for food on the rough sea floor.

SEALS AND SEA LIONS

Seals and sea lions are mammals, but have bodies adapted to life in the water. They spend much of their time underwater, and are skillful swimmers and divers. They breathe air, but being heavy and ungainly, do not move so freely on land.

FANTASTIC FACT

The heartbeat of the seal and the walrus slows down underwater to help stop them running out of air.

Northern fur seal

Northern fur seals have large rear flippers and feed on fish or squid. Male seals may be four times the size of females. Females stay with their young for seven days before going off briefly to feed, then return to feed their pups from rich milk.

Northern fur seals rarely come to land except to breed.

California sea lions are the fastest swimmers of all the seals and sea lions.

California sea lion

California sea lions can swim at speeds of up to 25 miles per hour, and can move fast on land by turning their back flippers forward and lifting their bodies. Huge colonies of sea lions gather on the rocky southwestern shores of the USA.

Leopard seal

The leopard seal is the fiercest hunter of all seals, preying on penguins and catching them underwater, just as they leave the pack ice of the Antarctic. It also hunts smaller seals as well as fish, squid, and shellfish.

Leopard seals have large jaws studded with teeth for tearing prey.

On land, walruses are very heavy and move with great difficulty.

Walrus

Walruses are large animals that live in the Arctic, where they feed on shellfish. Walruses have sharp tusks, which they use to fight and to drag themselves out of the water. Their thick skins protect them from injury and they are excellent swimmers.

BEES AND WASPS

Bees and wasps are brightly colored invertebrate insects. Insects have a head, a middle part called the **thorax**, a lower part called the **abdomen**, and three pairs of legs. Bees and wasps have a narrow waist where the thorax joins the abdomen.

Bee and wasp types

There are as many as 200,000 different species of bees and wasps, but only about 50,000 have been identified. The smallest are tiny parasitic wasps, and the largest are hornets. The most aggressive bee is the Africanized honeybee.

FANTASTIC FACT

Honeybees flap their wings more than 230 times per second. This makes the buzzing noise.

All wasps and bees, like this honeybee, have two pairs of wings.

Hornets can grow up to one inch in length.

118

Bees

Honeybees and bumblebees are the most common types of bee. They are social bees and live in large groups called colonies. Each member of the colony has a specific job to do. Most other species of bees live alone and are solitary.

Paper wasps chew up wood to make a sort of papier-mache for building their nests.

Wasps

Wasps can also be divided into social and solitary species. Social wasps include the common wasps, paper wasps and hornets. The potter, digger and parasitic wasps are all solitary wasps. Wasps use their stings to catch their prey—insects and spiders.

LIFE IN THE COLONY

In a honeybee colony, there are three types of bee: drones, workers, and queens. The queen is the largest bee and lays eggs. Drones are large male bees; they have no sting, and their only job is to mate with the queen. The majority are worker bees.

Worker bees build the combs from wax produced by their own body.

Worker bees

Young worker bees care for the queen, remove waste, build the nest and guard its entrance. Nurse bees feed and take care of the bee larvae. Older worker bees are called foragers, and collect nectar, pollen and water.

Bees' nests

Bees build nests with hanging structures made of wax, called combs. These contain cells, which are filled with eggs, larvae, **pupae**, and supplies of pollen and honey. The nest grows as more and more combs are added.

These worker honeybees are filling cells with pollen collected from flowers.

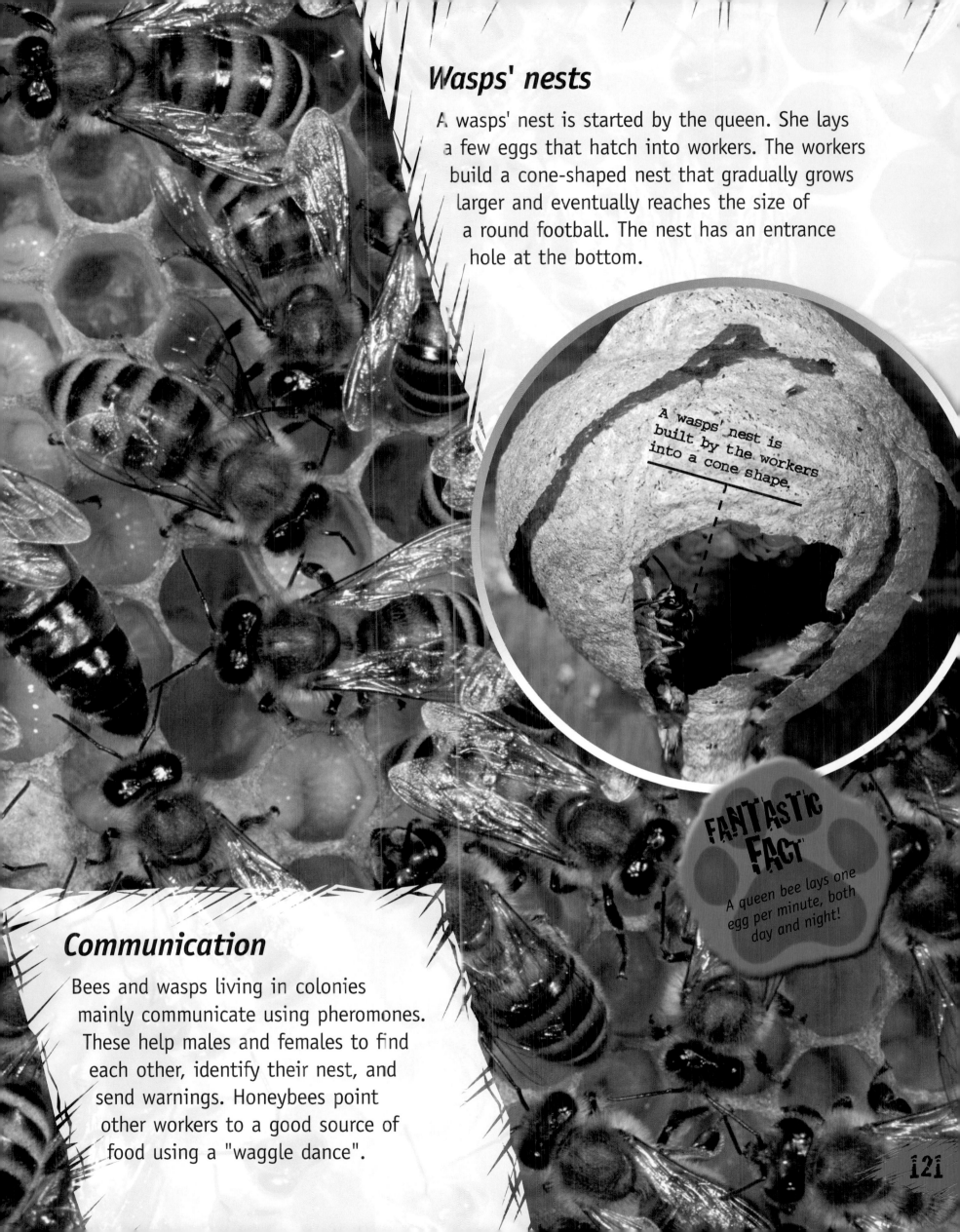

Wasps' nests

A wasps' nest is started by the queen. She lays a few eggs that hatch into workers. The workers build a cone-shaped nest that gradually grows larger and eventually reaches the size of a round football. The nest has an entrance hole at the bottom.

A wasps' nest is built by the workers into a cone shape.

FANTASTIC FACT

A queen bee lays one egg per minute, both day and night!

Communication

Bees and wasps living in colonies mainly communicate using pheromones. These help males and females to find each other, identify their nest, and send warnings. Honeybees point other workers to a good source of food using a "waggle dance".

SPIDERS

Large tarantulas may grow out of their exoskeleton 40 times in their lives.

Spiders belong to a group of animals called arachnids. Arachnids have four pairs of legs, eight eyes, a pair of fangs and a two-part body. Instead of bones, they have an **exoskeleton**. Scorpions, mites, and ticks also belong to the arachnid family.

Types of spider

There are at least 40,000 species of spider, ranging from five inch long tarantulas to tiny money spiders less than a half inch long. One of the largest groups is the jumping spiders. Other groups include orb web spiders, which spin a circular web of silk.

Jumping spiders lie in wait and then leap onto their prey.

FANTASTIC FACT

The largest spider in the world is the goliath bird-eating spider. It measures 12 inches across when its legs are stretched out!

122

Raft spiders live in marshy places and can run across the water's surface.

Where do you find spiders?

Spiders are found in almost all areas of the world. The only places that spiders do not live are the cold polar regions. Most spiders are found in forests, woodland, and grassland, but some live in caves and deserts. A few spiders live on or in water.

To stretch out or raise a leg, a spider must pump fluid into it from its body.

Fast runners

Spiders can run quickly because of their seven-part jointed leg structure, making them much more flexible than our legs. Contracting muscles move their legs toward their body, but they have no muscles to move their legs back out again.

SPECIAL SPIDER SKILLS

Orb web spiders weave webs across open spaces to trap flying insects.

Spiders collect information from their surroundings for protection and to catch their prey. They use their sensitive hairs and eight eyes which provide good sight.

Spinning webs

Spiders have special silk glands in their abdomen. They leave long, dry threads called draglines behind them as they move around. Spiders make a different, sticky silk to trap insects. As the prey struggles to escape, spiders feel these vibrations and rush in.

Silk becomes a solid thread as it is released.

Sensitive hairs

Most of the hairs on a spider's body are connected to nerves. The hairs pick up vibrations and air movement on the web and in their surroundings. Spiders can walk on ceilings and over glass because of a collection of short hairs on their feet.

Through each hair, a spider senses changes in air movement and in surroundings.

FANTASTIC FACT

Most spiders live for one or two years, but large female tarantulas can live up to 20!

Growing bigger

Spiders have an outer armored layer called an exoskeleton. To grow bigger, they have to **molt**. The old exoskeleton loosens and splits open, and the spider climbs out. The new exoskeleton is soft while the spider stretches its body, then it hardens.

ANTS

There are more ants in the world than any other type of insect. They live in large groups called colonies. Their most important sense organs are in their **antennae**, which they use for feeling and smelling. An ant's **compound eyes** see poorly.

These leafcutter ants are carrying bits of leaves back to the colony.

This harvester ant has found a large seed.

Types of ant

There are about 10,000 named species of ant. The largest are the driver ants; their queens can be up to nearly two inches long. The smallest is the pharaoh ant, no bigger than a grain of sand. Ants are grouped by how they look, what they eat, and where they live.

Where do you find ants?

Ants can survive in hot deserts, but they cannot live in very cold areas, such as Antarctica, Iceland, and Greenland. They are also not found on some Pacific Ocean islands. The largest colonies are found in tropical rainforests.

Desert ants can survive on hot sand that reaches temperatures of 158°F.

What do ants eat?

Ants eat many sorts of food, including seeds and rotting fruit on the ground. Ants also feed on insects, small spiders, and tiny worms. Ants cannot chew. Instead they have powerful jaws for gripping and squeezing the liquid out of the food.

The jaws of soldier ants are huge. They use them to defend the colony.

127

COLONY LIFE

Ants live in colonies of many different sizes, from small groups to huge ones. A colony of black ants will contain about 400 ants, while a wood ant colony has 300,000 or more ants. Some colonies are made up of millions of ants.

Army and driver ants hold onto each other to build temporary nests called bivouacs.

Workers and queens

Female workers in a colony build the nest, gather food, look after the eggs, and feed the larvae. There is usually one queen that lays all the eggs. Male ants are only found in the colony at certain times of the year. They mate with the queen and then die.

Ants' nests

Many ants make nests underground. Carpenter ants carve out rooms and tunnels in rotting wood, while Aztec ants nest in a living tree trunk. Army and driver ants have no permanent nests. They form a living curtain around the queen, eggs, and larvae.

Tailor ants use sticky thread to glue leaves together, forming a nest in a tree.

Winged ants often emerge from the ground on warm summer evenings.

Flying ants

At certain times of the year, winged ants appear. These are the new queens and males. They need wings to fly away and start a new colony. After mating, the males die. Then the queen chews off her wings and goes underground to lay eggs for a new colony.

129

BUTTERFLIES

Butterflies are colorful winged insects. They do not start life this way. Young butterflies are called caterpillars. Caterpillars eat all the food they can, and then pupate, when the caterpillar changes into a butterfly. This is known as **metamorphosis**.

FANTASTIC FACT

The monarch butterfly may fly more than 80 miles in a single day!

The largest and brightest butterflies, like this blue morpho, live in rainforests.

Peacock butterflies are often seen in flower-filled meadows.

Where can you find butterflies?

Butterflies are found in almost every habitat where there are plenty of flowers, from warm tropical areas to colder northern areas near the Arctic. There are no butterflies in the coldest parts of the world, such as the Antarctic.

Butterfly senses

Adult butterflies have compound eyes. They can see small movements and also colors. Butterflies have long antennae for picking up smells, and they have taste buds on their feet! This helps the females to find plants to lay her eggs on.

This green birdwing butterfly is tasting a plant using taste buds on its feet.

Butterfly wings

A butterfly has two pairs of wings. The upper and lower wings are hooked together so they move as one. Most butterflies do not fly far, but some, like the monarch butterfly, migrate thousands of miles.

The colors on butterfly wings come from light reflected by wing scales.

CATERPILLARS AND PUPAE

Caterpillars look nothing like the adult butterfly. Caterpillars do nothing but eat plants and grow, while adult butterflies can only drink nectar. Many butterflies that are poisonous to predators get this poison from plants the have eaten as caterpillars.

Growing caterpillars

Like all insects, caterpillars have a tough outer covering that does not stretch. As the caterpillar grows, this covering gets too small and the caterpillar molts. This happens about five times, at which point the caterpillar reaches its full size and becomes a pupa.

Like all caterpillars, this swallowtail's body is made of many segments.

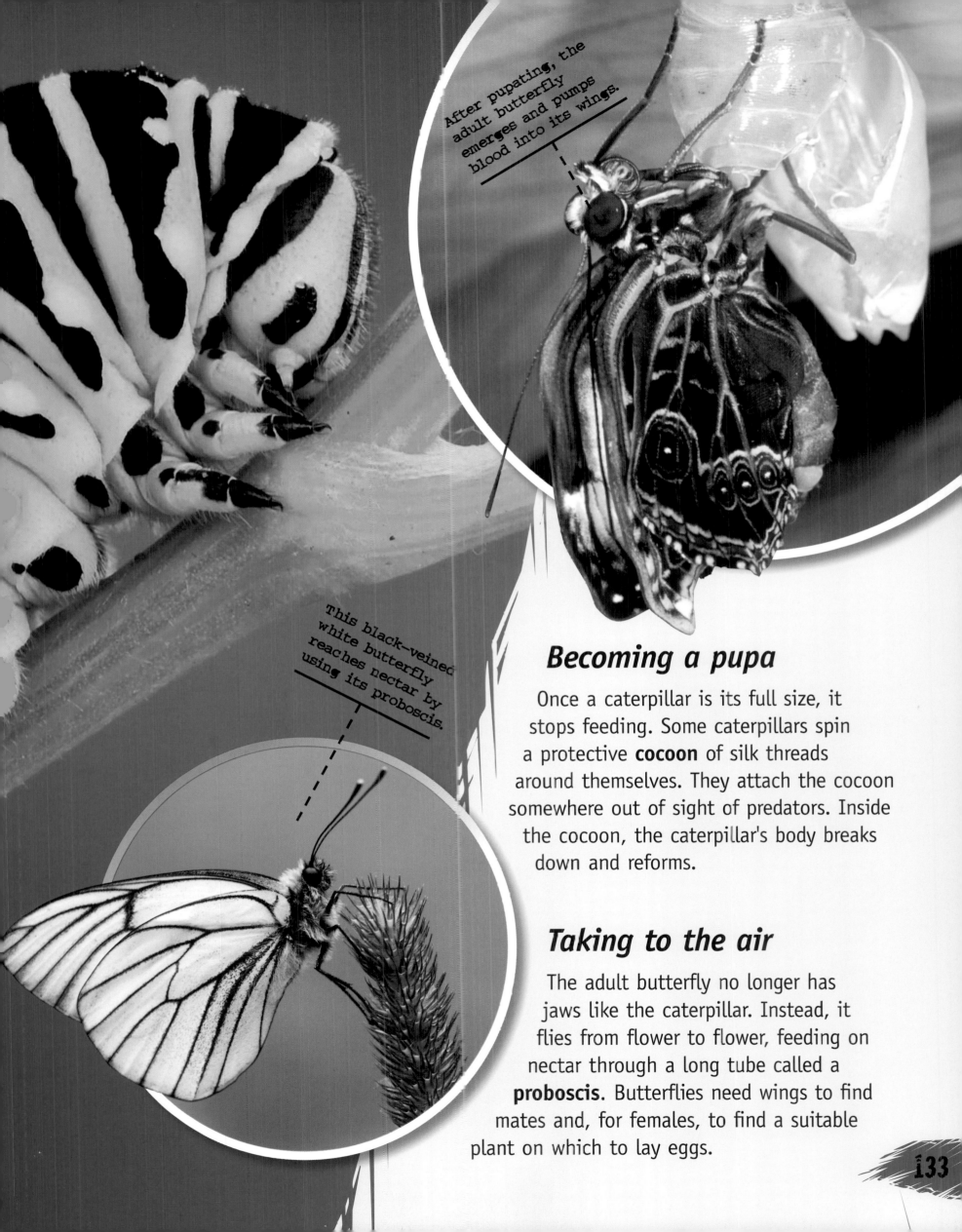

After pupating, the adult butterfly emerges and pumps blood into its wings.

This black-veined white butterfly reaches nectar by using its proboscis.

Becoming a pupa

Once a caterpillar is its full size, it stops feeding. Some caterpillars spin a protective **cocoon** of silk threads around themselves. They attach the cocoon somewhere out of sight of predators. Inside the cocoon, the caterpillar's body breaks down and reforms.

Taking to the air

The adult butterfly no longer has jaws like the caterpillar. Instead, it flies from flower to flower, feeding on nectar through a long tube called a **proboscis**. Butterflies need wings to find mates and, for females, to find a suitable plant on which to lay eggs.

133

MANTIDS AND DRAGONFLIES

Flower mantis

The flower mantis has two long, grasping forelegs. It has have compound eyes with very good eyesight, to spot insect prey. Most have two sets of wings. The outer wings are narrow and leathery. Only the transparent inner wings are for flying.

Mantids, dragonflies, and their relatives are some of the fiercest insect predators. Mantids are expert hunters, grasping their prey with long front legs. Dragonflies are some of the fastest-flying of all insects, and seize their prey in the air.

FANTASTIC FACT

Flower mantises are the only insects able to turn their heads 180 degrees.

Different species of flower mantis are colored to match the flowers they perch on.

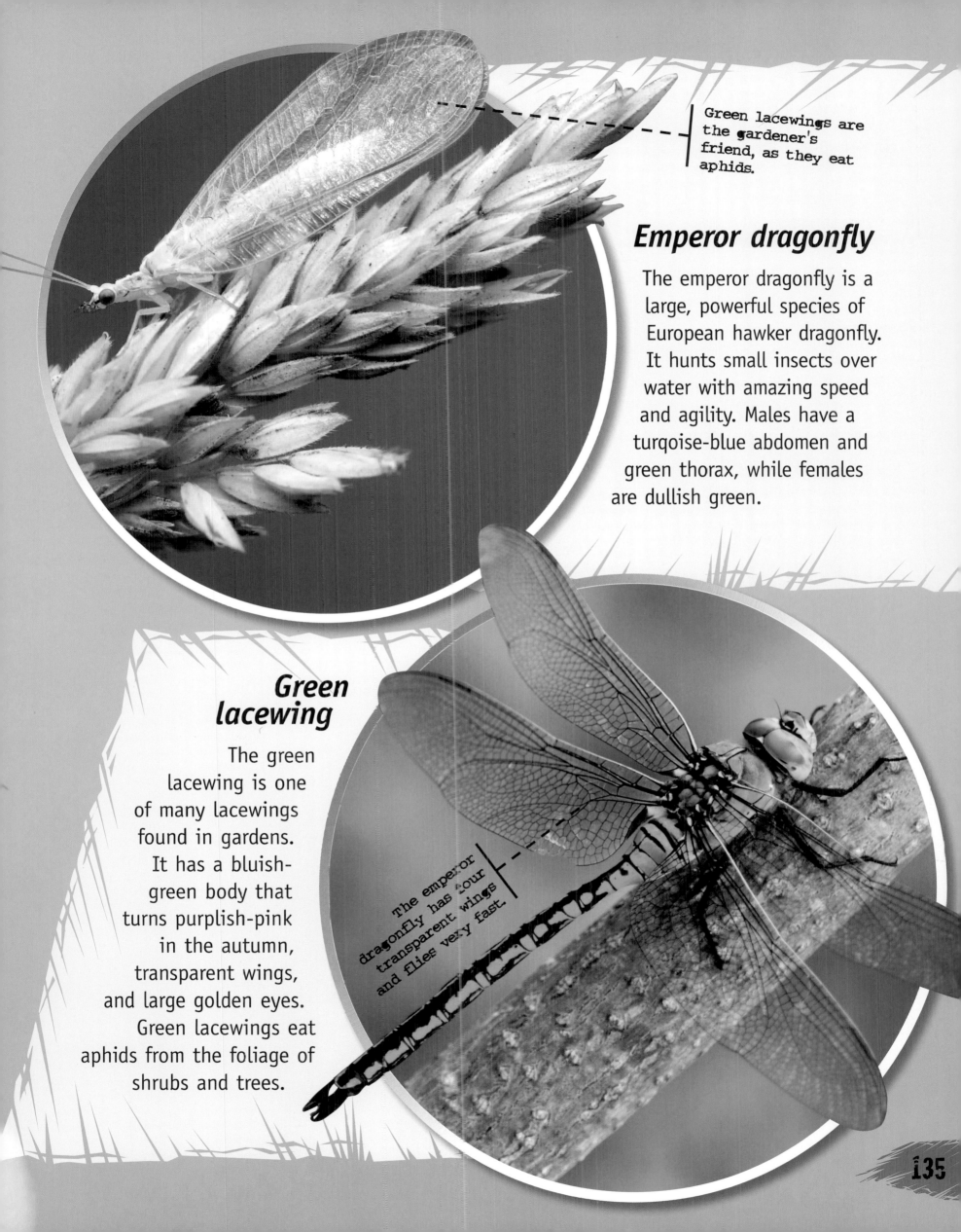

Green lacewings are the gardener's friend, as they eat aphids.

Emperor dragonfly

The emperor dragonfly is a large, powerful species of European hawker dragonfly. It hunts small insects over water with amazing speed and agility. Males have a turqoise-blue abdomen and green thorax, while females are dullish green.

Green lacewing

The green lacewing is one of many lacewings found in gardens. It has a bluish-green body that turns purplish-pink in the autumn, transparent wings, and large golden eyes. Green lacewings eat aphids from the foliage of shrubs and trees.

The emperor dragonfly has four transparent wings and flies very fast.

BEETLES

Beetles form the largest group of insects. More than 250,000 species are known. Beetles live almost everywhere, from polar regions to rainforests. They eat many types of food. Some hunt insects, while others eat seeds. Some even eat dung.

Diving beetle

Diving beetles live in freshwater ponds and streams. They swim by moving their long back legs like oars. Both adults and larvae hunt prey—the larvae can catch tadpoles. Diving beetles also fly at night in spring and autumn, looking for new ponds.

Diving beetles are found all over the world except in the Arctic Circle.

Rhinoceros beetle

The rhinoceros beetle is one of the largest beetles. Male beetles use their horns to forage through leaf litter on the jungle floor, to fight other males and to dig a burrow.

FANTASTIC FACT

Rhinoceros beetles are one of the strongest animals known. They can lift up to 850 times their own weight!

Male rhinoceros beetles have spectacular horns.

Click beetles leap into the air to right themselves or to escape predators.

Click beetle

Click beetles make a clicking sound as they leap into the air to avoid predators. They live everywhere except in the Arctic Circle. Some click beetles are very colorful, but most are brown or black. The larvae, called wireworms, attack the roots of crops.

Firefly

More than 2,000 species of firefly are known, living in temperate and tropical habitats around the world. Fireflies produce a yellowish light from a special area at the end of the abdomen. Each species flashes its light in a particular pattern to attract mates.

Male fireflies have wings, but female fireflies do not.

SCORPIONS AND MITES

Some scorpion stings can kill a human, but most are no worse than a wasp sting.

Scorpions, like spiders, belong to the arachnid family. They use a venomous sting to kill prey and defend themselves. The arachnid group also includes tiny mites and ticks. Most mites prey on other insects, while ticks feed on mammal blood.

Scorpion

The scorpion is a fierce hunter. It is armed with large pincers for grasping its prey, and has a venomous stinger at the end of its body to inject the prey with venom. Scorpions hide under stones or logs during the day, and hunt insects and spiders at night.

FANTASTIC FACT

Scorpions have been around for hundreds of millions of years, before dinosaurs roamed the Earth.

House dust mite

Dust mites live in mattresses, carpets, furniture, and bedding, and are a common cause of asthma in humans. Dust mites live on tiny particles of organic matter. Some species prefer skin cells, a major part of household dust. Other species prefer flour dust.

House dust mites are tiny, only 0.25–0.5mm long.

Tick

There are two main types of ticks, hard-bodied and soft-bodied. Ticks live in long grass and on bushes. They do not jump or fly, but wait for a warm-blooded animal to brush past. Ticks bite the host animal so they can feed on the blood.

Ticks are found everywhere except in regions that are permanently cold.

139

GLOSSARY

abdomen
the third part of an insect's body, behind the thorax

amphibian
an animal with a skeleton that lives both on land and in water, usually laying its eggs in water.

antennae
feelers on an insect's head that detect smells in the air

blowhole
the large nostril of a whale, dolphin, or porpoise, on top of its head

blubber
a thick layer of insulating fat under the skin

camouflage
markings or body shape that blend in with the surroundings to hide an animal

carnivore
an animal that eats only meat

cocoon
a case made of silk to protect spider eggs or a metamorphosing butterfly

colony
a group of animals living together

compound eyes
large eyes made up of many parts

echolocation
a special ability to map out surroundings using sound

exoskeleton
the hard outer covering that protects the body of an animal without a skeleton

gills
feathery structures an animal uses to get oxygen to breathe underwater

habitat
the place where an animal or plant lives

herbivore
an animal that eats only plant matter

incubate
to keep eggs warm until they are ready to hatch

insect
an animal with a three-part body and six legs

krill
seafood made up of many tiny shrimp-like animals that swim together in groups

larva (plural larvae)
the growing stage between the egg and the adult

mammal
an animal that gives birth to live young rather than eggs. Female mammals produce milk for their young.

melon
a structure in the forehead of a dolphin or porpoise, used for echolocation

metamorphosis
a change of body shape between the larva and adult stages

migration
a long journey made regularly by some animals to find better seasonal conditions

milk teeth
the name given to the first set of teeth a mammal has. These fall out and are replaced by larger adult teeth.

molting
when a bird replaces old feathers with new ones, or an old exoskeleton is replaced .

nectar
the sugary liquid produced by many flowers

plankton
tiny plants or animals that float in great numbers in the ocean

predator
an animal that hunts other animals as prey

primate
a type of mammal, such as a monkey, ape, or human, with hands and feet and a large brain

proboscis
the feeding tube certain insects have instead of a mouth

pupa (plural pupae)
the stage when a larva changes into an adult

141

GLOSSARY

rainforest
dense forest with very heavy rainfall, found in hot and wet areas of the world

reptile
an animal with a skeleton, scaly skin, and body temperature controlled by its surroundings, which usually lays eggs

scale
a hard flake that is attached to the skin of a reptile, fish, or insect

species
a group of animals that look alike and can breed together to produce young

territory
the area in which an animal spends its life, and where it finds food and water

thermal
a current of warm air rising from the Earth's surface

thorax
the second part of an insect's body, joining the head to the abdomen

tropical
the parts of the world near the Equator that are hot all year round

venom
poison produced by some animals to disable prey and with which they defend themselves